NANCY

ART
of the
Palate

A COOKBOOK BY THE
PENINSULA FINE ARTS CENTER
ILLUSTRATED BY NANCY THOMAS

Great **CHEFS**

Great **RECIPES**

Great **FOOD**

All withstand the **TEST** of **TIME**

The Greats **ALWAYS DO**

THE
OLD
POINT
NATIONAL
BANK
Progressive Banking Since 1923.
All Offices
(757) 728-1200
www.oldpoint.com

WIMMER
COOKBOOKS

A CONSOLIDATED GRAPHICS COMPANY

800.548.2537   wimmerco.com

TABLE OF CONTENTS

BETTY SCOTT YANCEY WASH

Art and food—the perfect pairing—and the perfect way to remember Betty Scott Yancey Wash. Betty's love of food was learned from her mother's kitchen and generously shared with an entire community through treasured recipes and deliciously prepared meals. As a young woman, Betty majored in art at Hollins College and spent the rest of her life collecting, enjoying and encouraging artists in a wide variety of media.

The formation of the Peninsula Fine Arts Center was a dream come true for Betty and from its inception she became one of its most enthusiastic supporters. As a board member, no job was too large or too small, but Betty's particular passion was serving for over twenty years as the buyer of the Gallery Shop and the annual holiday event, "Artful Giving."

For those who knew and loved Betty Wash this book is a celebration of two of her lifetime passions, and it is with pride that her family remembers her through this book.

INTRODUCTION

Introducing a cookbook that's as attractive as it is delicious. The reason is nationally known contemporary artist Nancy Thomas, who brings her charming personality and colorful talent to Art of the Palate. Nancy is a total delight and you'll feel as if you're talking with a good friend as she tells you stories of her adventures with food, her childhood, her travels, restaurants and meals she loves, and what it feels like to be an artist. Throughout the book, her comments will amuse you, her tips enlighten you and her original cover and divider paintings capture the art of the palate...and the palette.

Like so many of us, Nancy Thomas loves to celebrate gatherings around the table. Her friends include chef Marcel DeSaulniers, with whom she created the book, Alphabet of Sweets. She created the official painting for Julia Child's 90th birthday, commissioned by the International Association of Culinary Professionals, and presented it to the legendary chef. And reproductions of her classic "Bon Appetit" painting have achieved several million dollars in sales.

Collaborating with the Peninsula Fine Arts Center, Nancy Thomas has worked with its staff and volunteers to create Art of the Palate to benefit the Center and its programs for years. Fully adhering to the Center's belief that "art is what you make it," Art of the Palate recognizes art as pulling perfectly roasted salmon fillets out of the oven, or presenting sweet little chocolate cream pots for dessert. Each recipe is twice-tested, featuring fresh ingredients and easy-to-follow directions.

Enjoy this special cookbook filled with art, personality and recipes. It's truly a feast for all your senses and a celebration of the creative experience.

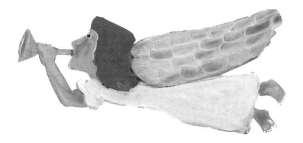

The profits from the sale of this book directly benefit the Peninsula Fine Arts Center and its ongoing mission of art education and the enrichment of the communities it serves.

ANGELS WITH A HEART
ART OF THE PALATE SPONSORS

Good Hopes Angel
Dr. Thomas A. Wash

Golden Charger Angel
Old Point National Bank

Silver Ladle Angel
Shirley A. Hatten

Copper Spoon Angels

Bay Community Bank

Rona M. and Erwin B. Drucker Charitable Trust

Rose and John Garrett

Quincy and Mary Sherwood Holt

Lockwood Brothers, Inc.

Parks Orthodontics

Dr. William R. Parks

Dr. Meredith S. Parks

RBC Centura

Riverside Health System

Bon Appetit Angels

Mary Henley and Leroy Thompson

Sue Anne and Bill Bangel; Joanne and William T. Roos

Wendy C. Drucker and Michael Piercy

Vicki and Bobby Freeman

Anne and William Hart

Drs. Carol and John Hogg

Mr. and Mrs. Jeffrey Luckman

Mr. and Mrs. David Peebles

Pfac Guild

Nancy M. Phillips

In Memory of H. Franklin Phillips

Judy and Gayle Rauch

Tzina and Louis Richman, Jr.

Barbara and Neal Rosenbaum

Ron Staples Custom Builder

Virginia Health Services

Celebration Angels

Carmines, Robbins and Company, PLC-CPA's

Joan Aaron

Ettalea Kanter

Sarfan & Nachman Attorneys

Walter and Ann Segaloff

Farm Fresh Charitable Trust

Angels Among Us

The Warwick Cheese Shoppe, for wine pairings

Raoust + Partners, for advance marketing publications

Celebrations

CELEBRATIONS

SUMMER

OFF TO THE BEACH

Rosemary Cayenne Walnuts

Sherry

Curried Vegetable Dip with an
Assortment of Summer Vegetables

Blanc de Noir Frizzante

Mediterranean Tuna Sandwiches

Laura's La La Salad

White Chocolate Brownies

DINNER ON THE TERRACE

Herbed Goat Cheese with Crackers

Sancerre

Corn, Avocado, and Tomato Salad

Herbed Flank Steak with Pink Pickled Onions

Merlot

Green Beans with Feta Cheese

Scrumptious Berry Cobbler

FALL

IT'S A KICK

 *Codornia Cava*

Chipotle Pecan Cheese Spread with Crackers

Tailgate Sandwiches

Potato Leek Soup

Lentil Salad

Featherweight Peanut Butter Cookies

VIRGINIA DINNER

Dilled Crabmeat on Cayenne Toasts

 *Gerüwrztraminer*

Butternut Squash and Apple Soup

Southern Biscuits

Spice Crusted Ham with Maple Mustard Sauce

 *Côtes de Provence*

Spinach, Granny Smith, and Cheddar Cheese Salad

Ginger Lime Sweet Potatoes

Pan Browned Brussels Sprouts

Cream Cheese Pound Cake

WINTER

DINNER BY THE FIRE

Feta, Olive, and Red Pepper Gratin with Pita Chips

Santorini

Creamy Mushroom Soup

Farmers Potatoes

Balsamic Gingered Lamb Shanks

Château-Neuf-du-Pâpe

Grilled Pear Salad with Port Vinaigrette

Chocolate Raspberry Pudding Cake

THE CELEBRATION TABLE

Fig and Walnut Tapennade with Goat Cheese

Sauvignon Blanc

Tidewater Crab Spread

Gingered Carrot Coup with Chives and Crème Fraîche

Grilled Dijon-Pepper Rib Roast with
Sour Cream Horseradish Sauce

Pomerol

Spinach Gratin

Herb Glazed Onions

Devilish Potatoes

Chocolate Chunk Celebrations

SPRING

VIRGINIA GARDEN WEEK LUNCHEON

 Chardonnay

Laura's Cheesy Snack Crackers

Asparagus Soup with Lemon Cream

Aspen Salad

Cheese Biscuits

Frozen Chocolate Mint Velvets

DAFFODIL DINNER

Curried Cheese Ball with Gingersnaps

 Gewürztraminer

Citrus Shrimp

Cream of Watercress Soup

Poached Salmon with Herbed Aïoli

 Chassagne Montrachet

Asparagus Gratin with Parmesan Cheese

Jasmine Rice Pilaf

Herbed Pita Toasts

Strawberries with Brown Sugar
and Balsamic Vinegar

Appetizers

APPETIZERS

DILLED CRABMEAT ON CAYENNE TOASTS

TOASTS
6	slices firm white sandwich bread
3	tablespoons unsalted butter
⅛	teaspoon cayenne
¼	teaspoon salt

CRABMEAT MIXTURE
6	ounces jumbo lump crabmeat
1	tablespoon minced shallots
1	tablespoon chopped fresh dill leaves
2	tablespoons mayonnaise
2	tablespoons sour cream
2	teaspoons fresh lemon juice
	Salt to taste
	Dill sprigs for garnish

Dill, the herbs, and the cayenne call for a Gewürztraminer. The best: J.B. Adams; the frugal alternative: Covey Run

To make toasts, preheat oven 350°. Stack bread slices and cut off crusts. Quarter slices to make twenty-four 1½-inch squares and arrange squares on baking sheet. In a small saucepan melt butter and stir in cayenne and salt. Brush tops of squares with butter mixture and bake about 10 minutes in middle of oven until pale golden. Cool toasts on rack. Toasts may be made 1 day ahead and kept in an airtight container at room temperature. To prepare crabmeat, pick over crab to remove any bits of shell and cartilage, being careful not to break up lumps. In a bowl, stir together remaining ingredients with salt to taste and gently stir in crab. This mixture may be made 6 hours ahead and chilled, covered. Just before serving, mound about ½ tablespoon of crab mixture on each toast and garnish with dill.

Yield: 24 canapés

TIDEWATER CRAB SPREAD

1	tablespoon milk
1	(8-ounce) package cream cheese, softened
8	ounces lump crabmeat
2	tablespoons minced green onion
½	teaspoon horseradish
¼	teaspoon salt, optional
	Pepper to taste
	Dash of hot pepper sauce
⅓	cup sliced almonds, toasted
	Crackers

Preheat oven to 350°. In a large bowl, blend together milk and cream cheese. Mix in the crab, onion, horseradish, salt, pepper sauce, and onions. Transfer into an ovenproof dish and sprinkle top with almonds. Bake in oven until hot and bubbly. Serve with crackers.

Yield: 8-10 servings

The almonds, onions, and horseradish suggest a Sauvignon Blanc. The best: Quivra; the frugal alternative: Snoqualamie

CRABMEAT MELTAWAYS

12	English muffins
2	(5-ounce) jars sharp processed cheese spread
¾	cup margarine
1	pound lump crabmeat
3	tablespoons mayonnaise
	Garlic salt to taste

Preheat broiler. Slice muffins in half. Melt cheese and margarine in microwave; add crabmeat, mayonnaise, and garlic salt. Spread mixture on muffins and cut into 4 triangles. Broil in oven until slightly browned

Cook's Note: *May be frozen on cookie sheets and then packaged for freezer. Broil slightly thawed triangles when ready to serve.*

Yield: 8 dozen

Cheddar and Chardonnay, no question! The best: Louis Jadot Meursault; the frugal alternative: Milton Park.

CITRUS SHRIMP

1½	pounds large shrimp
1½	cups orange juice
	Juice and zest of 1 lime
1	(14-ounce) bottle clam broth
	Zest of 1 orange
1	teaspoon ground cumin
1	teaspoon ground cardamom
¼	teaspoon cayenne pepper
	Salt and black pepper to taste

Rinse shrimp, peel and devein. Set aside. In a medium saucepan, combine the rest of the ingredients. Bring mixture to a boil and stir in shrimp. Cover and cook 3 minutes or just until shrimp begins to curl and turn pink. Remove from heat. Chill shrimp in cooking liquid. LET STAND at least 24 hours. Serve with cocktail and/or tartar sauce.

Yield: 24-30 pieces

Lime, cumin, and shrimp call for a Riesling. The best: Schloss Vollrads Kabinett; the frugal alternative: Columbia Crest.

MARINATED MUSHROOMS

1	pound fresh mushrooms
2	tablespoons lemon juice
¼	cup olive oil
1	tablespoon minced fresh parsley
½	teaspoon salt
½	teaspoon granulated sugar
½	cup cider vinegar
1	tablespoon oregano
1	tablespoon minced onion
1	clove garlic, minced

In a medium saucepan, place mushrooms in water with lemon juice. Bring to a boil, lower heat and simmer for 1 minute. Drain. Combine mushrooms and remaining ingredients. Put in a jar and refrigerate.

Cook's Note: *Serve in a colorful bowl or as part of a vegetable platter.*

Yield: 8-10 servings

Mushrooms pair well with Pinot Noir or Tempranillo. The best: Ebano Ribera del Duero; the frugal alternative: Protocollo.

14

Select a red and Rhône-like wine. The best: Domaine de Pegau Châteauneuf-du-Pâpe; the frugal alternative: Smoking Loon Syrah.

COUNTRY FRENCH PÂTÉ

½	cup unsalted butter
½	cup coarsely chopped shallots
2	cloves garlic, finely chopped
I	teaspoon dried tarragon
I	teaspoon dried rosemary, crumbled
¼	teaspoon dried thyme
¼	teaspoon ground savory
½	cup chopped leafy celery tops
12	black peppercorns
2	bay leaves
6	cups water
I	pound chicken livers, well rinsed
¼	teaspoon ground allspice
½	teaspoon salt
½	teaspoon freshly ground black pepper
¼	cup Madeira
	Parsley, chopped, for garnish

Melt butter in skillet over medium heat. Add the shallots, garlic, tarragon, rosemary, thyme, and savory and cook, covered, for 20 minutes. Combine celery tops, peppercorns, bay leaves, and water in a medium-size saucepan. Heat to boiling. Reduce heat and simmer, uncovered, 10 minutes. Add chicken livers to saucepan and simmer gently for 10 minutes. Do not overcook. Remove livers to a mixing bowl with a slotted spoon and discard remaining contents of saucepan. Add herb mixture, allspice, salt, pepper, and Madeira to the livers and mix well. Process the liver mixture in small batches in a food processor, fitted with a steel blade, until smooth. Remove mixture to a decorative 2-cup crock. Refrigerate covered at least 6 hours. Let the pâté warm at room temperature 30 minutes before serving. Garnish with parsley.

Yield: 2 cups

MARINATED BLACK AND GREEN OLIVES

2	cups small green olives
2	cups brine-cured black olives
2	small onions, sliced ½-inch thick
⅓	cup red wine vinegar
2	bay leaves
12	thyme sprigs or 1½ teaspoons dried, crumbled
1	teaspoon fennel seeds, crushed lightly with flat side of knife
2	teaspoons peppercorns
2	cups olive oil

In two saucepans of boiling water blanch green olives and black olives separately for 1 minute each and drain them in 2 sieves (do not mix olives). Divide onion between two 1-quart jars with tight-fitting lids. Pack green and black olives separately into jars while they are warm and divide mixture of vinegar, bay leaves, thyme, fennel, and peppercorns between the two jars, pushing thyme down into the mixture. Divide the oil between jars, seal with lids, and let stand in a cool, dark place, shaking daily for 3 days. Olives keep, covered and chilled, indefinitely. Mix the two olives when serving.

Yield: 4 cups

This dish calls for an Italian red. The best: Avignonesi Vino Nobile di Montepulciano; the frugal alternative: Cesanese de Piglio.

BLACK BEAN AND CORN SALSA

The jalapeños will tend to overpower anything. This dish calls for Encostas' do Lima Vinho Verde.

3	ears white corn
¾	cup water
3	medium tomatoes
2	jalapeño peppers
2	(12-ounce) cans black beans, rinsed and drained
1	cup chopped fresh cilantro
⅓	cup fresh lime juice
¼	teaspoon salt
¼	teaspoon freshly ground black pepper
2	avocados
	Tortilla chips

Cut corn from cob into a saucepan; add ¾ cup water, and bring to a boil. Cover, reduce heat, and simmer 6 to 7 minutes or until tender. Drain corn; transfer to a large bowl. Peel, seed, and finely chop tomatoes; add to corn. Seed and mince peppers; add to corn with beans and next 4 ingredients, stirring gently. Chill. Peel and finely chop avocados; stir into corn mixture, and serve chilled with tortilla chips.

Cook's Note: *May also be used as a side dish with Southwestern food.*

Yield: 8-10 servings

TOMATO-BASIL BRUSCHETTA

10	Roma tomatoes, chopped
3-6	scallions, chopped
½	cup chopped purple or Vidalia onion
¼-½	cup chopped fresh basil
2	teaspoons minced garlic
1	tablespoon olive oil
2	tablespoons balsamic vinegar
2	tablespoons white wine vinegar
1	tablespoon granulated sugar
¼	teaspoon salt
¼	teaspoon black pepper
1	(4-ounce) package feta cheese
	French bread rounds, toasted

Combine first 11 ingredients and mix well. Top with feta cheese and serve on toasted French bread rounds.

Yield: 2 dozen

The sweetness of the Vidalia onion, the basil, and the Roma tomatoes will pair with a slightly sweet sparking red wine. Try Tenuta Sanna Cabernet.

BACON TOMATO TARTS

1	package wonton wrappers
6	slices bacon, fried crisp and chopped
2	plum tomatoes, drained, coarsely chopped
½	small onion, chopped
½	cup mayonnaise
½	cup grated Swiss cheese
1	teaspoon dried basil

Preheat oven to 375°. Separate wonton wrappers and cut with small round cookie cutter. Place in mini-muffin tin and press into cups. In a bowl mix bacon and remaining ingredients. Blend well. Using a teaspoon put a small amount into cups. Bake about 10-15 minutes until golden brown.

Yield: 30 tarts

Bacon suggests a rosé. The best: Margan Shiraz Saignée; the frugal alternative: Norman White Zinfandel.

PARMESAN MUSHROOM CROUSTADES

36	slices white bread
3	tablespoons melted butter
3	tablespoons minced shallots
¼	cup butter
½	pound finely chopped mushrooms
2	tablespoons all-purpose flour
I	cup heavy cream
I½	tablespoons minced chives
I	tablespoon minced parsley
½	teaspoon lemon juice
½	teaspoon salt
⅛	teaspoon cayenne pepper
	Parmesan cheese

Nothing goes better with mushrooms and cream than Amontillado Sherry. Select Emilo Lustau Amontillado Sherry.

Preheat oven to 400°. With a biscuit cutter, cut a 3-inch round from each bread slice. Brush insides of 3 miniature muffin pans (12 muffin size) generously with melted butter. Gently fit the bread rounds into each mold to form a cup. Bake 10 minutes until lightly browned. Cool. For mushroom mixture, sauté shallots in butter for I minute in heavy skillet. Stir in mushrooms, cook uncovered about 10 minutes until all liquid has evaporated. Remove from heat, stir flour into mushrooms. Add cream and return to heat. Stirring constantly, bring to a boil, cook another minute or so while mixture becomes very thick. Remove from heat, stir in remaining ingredients. Cool, cover, and refrigerate until chilled. Preheat oven to 350°. Spoon mixture into the toast shells and sprinkle each with Parmesan cheese. Bake for 10 minutes and serve immediately.

Cook's Note: *After mixture is chilled, toast shells may be filled and frozen in their tins. Once frozen, remove to plastic bags for easier freezer storage. Thaw croustades (about 2 hours) on cookie sheet before baking.*

Yield: 36 croustades

GOAT CHEESE TAPENADE TARTS

- 12 baguette slices, ½-inch thick
- 3½ tablespoons extra virgin olive oil, divided
- 1 medium tomato, peeled, seeded, and cut into ¼-inch dice
- 2 tablespoons julienned soft sun-dried tomatoes
- 1 tablespoon torn fresh basil
- 1 teaspoon Sherry vinegar
- 2 tablespoons bottled black olive tapenade
- 8 ounces mild goat cheese log, softened, cut crosswise in ½-inch slices

Salt and black pepper

Torn fresh basil leaves for garnish

Preheat oven to 350°. Brush 1 side of baguette slices with 2 tablespoons oil and arrange, oiled sides up, on baking sheet. Toast bread about 7 minutes in middle of oven until golden on top. Transfer to rack to cool. Leave oven on. Stir together fresh and dried tomatoes, basil, vinegar, and ½ tablespoon oil. Spread each toast with tapenade and top with a slice of goat cheese and a rounded teaspoon of tomato mixture. Arrange on baking sheet, season with salt and pepper and drizzle with ½ tablespoon oil. Bake tarts about 5 minutes in middle of oven until cheese is softened. Transfer to a platter and drizzle with the remaining ½ tablespoon of oil.

Cook's Note: Toasts may be prepared 2 days ahead, cooled completely, and kept in airtight container at room temperature. Tomato mixture may be made 1 day ahead and chilled, covered.

Yield: 6 servings

I went to one of the James Beard dinners, which was extraordinary. It was just extraordinary! We sat at a big round table, and the centerpiece was wine glasses. There must have been a hundred wine glasses, because you had a wine at every course. So that was gorgeous looking, but then they would bring you your plate and you'd get a glass of wine and as the wine would go away, the centerpiece would disappear! It was all about food and wine, no flowers, nothing else, just that.

Choose a Sauvignon Blanc, a rich one but not fruity. The best: Philippe Raimbault Pouilly-Fumé: the frugal alternative: Montevina.

SPINACH CREAM CHEESE TART

CRUST
1	cup finely chopped onion
1	cup finely chopped pecans
1	cup shredded Cheddar cheese

FILLING
2	(10-ounce) packages frozen chopped spinach
1	(8-ounce) package cream cheese
1	(9-ounce) jar chutney
½	teaspoon ground nutmeg
½	teaspoon white pepper
½	teaspoon celery salt
	Crackers

Chutney requires a rich, but not sweet, Riesling. The best: Domaines Schlumberge; the frugal alternative: Schumann-Nagler Christopher-Philipp.

Blend crust ingredients and divide into 2 portions. Slightly oil a 7-inch springform pan; spread 1 portion of crust on bottom of pan. Press with spoon so that it is even. Thaw spinach completely and drain. Place on layers of paper towels, roll up, and squeeze until no more water comes out. In food processor blend spinach, chutney, nutmeg, pepper, and celery salt. Spread filling mixture over crust. Cover filling with remaining crust mixture. Apply light pressure with a spoon to the top crust to form the tart. Refrigerate overnight. Remove springform collar, cover the top with a serving plate and invert. Remove the pan bottom and chill until ready to serve with crackers.

Cook's Note: *For a larger tart, double the recipe and use a 9-inch springform pan.*

Yield: one 7-inch tart

BOLLITAS

- 1   cup shredded sharp Cheddar cheese
- 1   tablespoon unsalted butter, softened
- ¼   teaspoon paprika or cayenne pepper
- ½   cup all-purpose flour
- 24 garlic-jalapeño stuffed olives or other green stuffed olives, well-drained

Preheat oven to 400°. In bowl of food processor, combine cheese, butter, paprika and flour; process until mixture is smooth. Take about 1 tablespoon of the crumbly dough and place in the palm of your hand. Place an olive in the middle of the dough and wrap dough around olive. Place on baking sheet and cook for 15-20 minutes. Remove from oven and place on paper towel before serving.

Cook's Note: *These freeze well.*

Yield: 2 dozen

Pair the strength of jalapeño peppers with a Vinho Verde.

SUN-DRIED TOMATO CHEESECAKE

- 4   ounces sun-dried tomatoes packed in oil, drained (reserving oil), finely chopped
- 2   (8-ounce) packages cream cheese, softened
- ¼   cup grated Romano cheese
- 1   tablespoon reserved tomato oil
- ¼   cup chopped fresh basil
      Crackers or pita chips

Mix all ingredients in food processor. Cover and chill. Serve with crackers or pita chips.

Yield: 8-10 servings

Pick a great Italian red wine. The best: Vitae Brunello di Montalcino; the frugal alternative: Codirosso

LAURA'S CHEESY SNACK CRACKERS

½ cup butter, softened
2 cups shredded Cheddar cheese
1½ cups all-purpose flour
½ teaspoon salt
½ teaspoon cayenne pepper (optional)
1 tablespoon chopped chives or parsley

In large bowl, mix all ingredients together by hand. On a floured surface, roll out dough to about ¼-inch thick. Cut with cookie cutters into shapes. Sprinkle with more salt and cayenne if desired. Poke holes in crackers with toothpick. Bake in a 350° oven on an ungreased baking sheet for 12-15 minutes or until lightly browned. Cool completely.

Yield: 3 dozen

J. Lohr Cyprus Chardonnay would be a good selection.

My daughter, Laura, lived in Key West for five years. She would always take me to these out-of-the-way places. We went down this long road, down on a key, way, way down, right on the water. There was another little key right out there called Grover's Key. Well, Grover was an iguana who had his own table and who would come over and visit and get up and just sit at the bar!

SAVORY SALMON CHEESECAKE

CRUST
1	cup grated Parmesan cheese
1	cup breadcrumbs
½	cup butter, melted

CHEESECAKE
1	tablespoon olive oil
1	red onion, chopped
1	red bell pepper, chopped
½	green bell pepper, chopped, optional
½	teaspoon salt
¼	teaspoon freshly ground black pepper
28	ounces cream cheese, room temperature
4	eggs
1	teaspoon Creole seasoning
½	cup heavy cream
1	cup cubed smoked Gouda cheese
1	pound smoked salmon, cut into slivers

*Any Prosecco
would be good.
The best: N.V.
Rebuli, Prosecco
di Valdobbiadene.*

Preheat oven to 350°. To prepare crust, combine Parmesan, breadcrumbs and butter until thoroughly blended. Press mixture into bottom of 10-inch springform pan. Bake for 8 minutes. (May be prepared ahead and set aside). For cheesecake, heat oil in medium skillet over high heat. Add onions and bell peppers. Sauté for 2 minutes, stirring and shaking skillet. Stir in salt and pepper and continue cooking for 1 minute. Remove from heat. Using electric mixer, beat cream cheese with eggs until thick and frothy, (about 4 minutes). Add Creole seasoning, cream and vegetables. Beat until thoroughly mixed and creamy for 1-2 minutes. Fold in Gouda and salmon and beat 1 more minute. Pour filling over crust in springform pan. Bake for 1 hour 15 minutes or until firm. Allow to cool at least 2 hours before removing sides of pan. Chill before removing cheesecake from springform pan. Serve chilled or at room temperature.

Cook's Note: *Cheesecake keeps well in refrigerator and can be made 1 or 2 days before serving. Recipe can be halved and baked in 7-inch springform pan. Check for doneness of smaller pan after 50 minutes. Crab or shrimp may be substituted for salmon.*

Yield: 16-20 servings

ROSEMARY CAYENNE WALNUTS

2	tablespoons olive oil
I	tablespoon dried rosemary
I	teaspoon salt
½	teaspoon cayenne pepper
2	cups walnut halves or pieces

Preheat oven to 350°. In a medium bowl combine the first 4 ingredients. Add walnuts and toss to coat evenly with mixture. Spread on baking sheet and bake for 10 minutes, stirring after 5 minutes.

Yield: 2 cups

Try Tio Pepe Fino Sherry.

FETA, OLIVE, AND RED PEPPER GRATIN

½	pound feta, (preferably Greek), rinsed and drained
¼	teaspoon dried oregano, crumbled
¼	teaspoon black pepper
¼	cup drained bottled roasted red peppers, chopped
10	Kalamata or other brine-cured black olives, pitted, rinsed, chopped
2	tablespoons extra virgin olive oil
	Fresh flat-leaf parsley, chopped for garnish
	Pita wedges or crusty bread

Preheat broiler. Cut cheese into ½-inch thick slices and arrange in I layer in a large gratin or other shallow baking dish. Sprinkle with oregano and pepper. Stir together roasted peppers, olives, and oil in a small bowl; spoon mixture over and around cheese. Broil 2-4 inches from heat for about 5 minutes, until edges of cheese are golden. Garnish with parsley and serve with toasted pita wedges or crusty bread.

Yield: 4 servings

Select a Greek white wine such as Santorini.

CHILI CHEESE DIP

2 (8-ounce) packages cream cheese, softened
1 (15-ounce) can chili, no beans
2 (16-ounce) bottles medium salsa
2 scallions, chopped
8 ounces Monterey Jack cheese, grated
1 (4-ounce) can black chopped olives
 Tortilla chips

Preheat oven to 350°. Layer the ingredients in order. Bake for 30 minutes. Serve with tortilla chips.

Yield: 20 servings

Pair with Bonny Doon's Big House Red.

ATHENIAN ARTICHOKE DIP

1 (14-ounce) can artichoke hearts in water, drained, chopped
4 ounces feta cheese, chopped
¼ cup red or green bell pepper, chopped
1 clove garlic, pressed
1 cup mayonnaise
3 scallions with tops, thinly sliced
¾ teaspoon dried oregano leaves
¼ cup sliced almonds, optional

Preheat oven to 350°. Chop artichoke hearts, cheese and bell pepper; place in 1-quart bowl. Add pressed garlic, mayonnaise, green onion, and oregano. Mix well and spoon into 8-inch baking dish. Top with almonds, if desired. Bake 25-30 minutes or until golden brown and bubbly. Serve with pita chips or fresh vegetables.

Yield: 2½ cups

Select a dry Chenin Blanc such as Vinum or Dry Creek.

SHERRIED STILTON AND GREEN PEPPERCORN SPREAD

¾	pound Stilton cheese, crumbled and softened
6	ounces cream cheese, softened
2-3	tablespoons green peppercorns, packed in brine, drained
¼	cup medium-dry Sherry, or to taste
	Salt and black pepper

In a food processor blend the Stilton, cream cheese, peppercorns to taste, Sherry, salt, and pepper to taste until mixture is smooth. Transfer to crocks or ramekins. Serve with crackers.

Cook's Note: *Spread keeps for 1 week, covered and chilled.*

Yield: 2½ cups

Stilton pairs well with port, but this is an appetizer so pick a not too sweet Riesling. The best: Georg Albrecht Schneider Niersteiner Paterberg Riesling Kabinett; the frugal alternative: Peter Mertes Riesling.

BISTRO CHEESE SPREAD

2	cloves garlic, minced
8	ounces sweet unsalted whipped butter
2	(8-ounce) packages cream cheese
1½	teaspoons fresh basil, chopped
1	teaspoon salt
1½	teaspoons fresh marjoram, chopped
1½	teaspoons fresh chives, chopped
¾	teaspoon fresh thyme, chopped
¾	teaspoon freshly ground black pepper
3	teaspoons fresh dill, chopped

Place garlic in blender or food processor. Add butter, cream cheese and herbs. Mix well and chill before serving.

Yield: 3 cups

Pair with Graham Beck Brut Rosé.

CHIPOTLE PECAN CHEESE SPREAD

2	(8-ounce) packages light cream cheese, softened
I	cup shredded Cheddar cheese
3	scallions, finely chopped
3	chipotle peppers in adobo sauce
½	teaspoon Creole seasoning
½	teaspoon cumin
½	teaspoon chili powder
¼	teaspoon Worcestershire sauce
⅛	teaspoon hot pepper sauce
⅓	cup chopped pecans

In a food processor, combine all ingredients except pecans, pulse 3 times, stopping to scrape down sides. Stir in pecans and chill 2 hours. Serve with assorted crackers and/or vegetables.

Cook's Note: *Can be prepared up to 3 days ahead. Serve leftovers on sandwiches.*

Yield: 3 cups

Pick a Spanish sparkling wine such as Codorniu Cava.

HERBED GOAT CHEESE

I	tablespoon each of 3 of the following chopped fresh herbs: chives, parsley, lemon thyme, tarragon, or French thyme
I	tablespoon freshly ground black pepper
I	small log plain goat cheese

Mix herbs and pepper on a sheet of plastic wrap. Roll the goat cheese in the mixture, coating it well. Tightly roll up in plastic wrap and chill. Serve with crackers.

Yield: 10 servings

Try Guy Saget Sancerre

CURRIED CHEESE BALL WITH GINGERSNAPS

3	(8-ounce) packages cream cheese, softened
3	tablespoons brown sugar
3	tablespoons dry Sherry
1	tablespoon ground ginger
1	teaspoon dry mustard
3-4	scallions, chopped
6-8	ounces shredded Cheddar cheese
1-2	teaspoons curry
1½	cups dried, finely chopped apricots or toasted almond slivers
	Bottled chutney
	Thin gingersnaps

Mix first 8 ingredients well and form into a ball; cover with apricots or almonds. When ready to serve, drizzle with chutney. Serve with gingersnaps.

Yield: 1 large cheese ball

Select Covey Run
Gewürztraminer

FIG AND WALNUT TAPENADE WITH GOAT CHEESE

- 1 cup dried Calimyrna figs, stemmed, chopped
- ⅓ cup water
- ⅓ cup Kalamata olives, pitted, chopped
- 2 tablespoons extra virgin olive oil
- 1 tablespoon balsamic vinegar
- 1 tablespoon capers, drained, chopped
- 1½ teaspoons fresh thyme, chopped
  Salt and black pepper
- 2 (5½-ounce) logs soft fresh goat cheese, cut crosswise into ½-inch rounds
- ½ cup chopped, toasted walnuts

Combine chopped figs and ⅓ cup water in heavy medium saucepan. Cook about 7 minutes over medium-high heat until liquid evaporates and figs are soft. Transfer to medium bowl. Mix in olives, olive oil, balsamic vinegar, capers, and chopped thyme. Season tapenade to taste with salt and pepper. Cover and refrigerate. Bring to room temperature before serving. Arrange overlapping cheese rounds in circle in center of medium platter. Stir chopped walnuts into tapenade and spoon into center of cheese circle. Serve with bread or crackers.

Yield: 20 servings

Try Westbrook Sauvignon Blanc.

HONEY LIME FRUIT DIP

- ½ cup heavy cream
- 1 tablespoon honey
- 1 tablespoon fresh lime juice
- 2 teaspoons confectioners' sugar

Beat heavy cream with honey, lime juice and confectioners' sugar until thick and creamy. Serve with skewered fresh fruit.

Yield: ½ cup

Viognier pairs with the honey; Chardonnay lends the crisp taste. Select Laurent Miguel Chardonnay Viognier.

CURRIED VEGETABLE DIP

½ cup sour cream
¼ cup mayonnaise
3 ounces cream cheese, softened
1 teaspoon fresh lemon juice, or to taste
1 teaspoon curry powder
½ teaspoon ground cumin
½ teaspoon salt
¼ teaspoon turmeric
⅓ cup finely chopped celery
⅓ cup finely chopped peeled and seeded
    cucumber
1 scallion, trimmed and finely chopped
   Scallion greens, sliced diagonally or
    toasted, slivered almonds for garnish

Whisk together sour cream, mayonnaise, cream cheese, lemon juice, curry, cumin, salt, and turmeric until smooth, Stir in celery, cucumber, and chopped scallion. Garnish with scallion greens or slivered almonds. Serve with fresh vegetables.

Cook's Note: *Dip can be made 2 days ahead and chilled, covered.*

Yield: 1 ½ cups

A good pairing would be Mein Klang Blanc de Noir Frizzante

CASA GRANDE DIP OR DRESSING

2   scallions, chopped
1   cup sour cream
2   tablespoons mayonnaise
2-3 tablespoons fresh lemon juice
½   cup blue cheese

Combine all ingredients and chill for several hours. Serve as a dip with a variety of vegetables or on wedges of lettuce.

Yield: 1 ½ cups

Select a Riesling.

SUN-DRIED TOMATO SCALLION DIP

¼ cup sun-dried tomatoes in oil, drained and chopped
1 (8-ounce) package cream cheese, softened
½ cup sour cream
½ cup mayonnaise
10 dashes hot pepper sauce
½ teaspoon salt
¾ teaspoon freshly ground black pepper
2 scallions, thinly sliced (white and green parts), divided

In a food processor fitted with a metal blade, purée tomatoes, cream cheese, sour cream, mayonnaise, hot pepper sauce, salt, and pepper. Add half of the scallions and pulse twice. Place in a decorative bowl or crock, garnish with remaining scallions. Serve at room temperature with crackers, chips or fresh vegetables.

Yield: 2 cups

Try a Merlot-like wine such as Musaragno Malbec.

My mother and grandmother made delicious Deviled Eggs. They weren't fancy, just mayonnaise, mustard and pickle relish.

TZATZIKI

4	cups plain yogurt, whole milk or low-fat
2	hothouse cucumbers, unpeeled and seeded
2	tablespoons plus 1 teaspoon Kosher salt, divided
1	cup sour cream
2	tablespoons champagne or white wine vinegar
¼	cup freshly squeezed lemon juice (2 lemons)
2	tablespoons olive oil
1	tablespoon minced garlic
1	tablespoon minced fresh dill
½	teaspoon salt
¼	teaspoon freshly ground black pepper

A Greek white wine such as Santorini would be a good choice.

Place the yogurt in a cheesecloth-lined sieve and set over bowl. Grate cucumber and toss with 2 tablespoons salt; place it in another sieve and set over another bowl. Place both bowls in the refrigerator for 3 to 4 hours to drain. Transfer thickened yogurt to large bowl. Squeeze as much liquid from the cucumbers as possible and add the cucumbers to yogurt. Mix in sour cream, vinegar, lemon juice, olive oil, garlic, dill, salt, and pepper. Serve immediately or allow the tzatziki to sit in refrigerator for a few hours for flavors to blend. Serve with pita as a dip or over grilled fish as a salsa.

Yield: 5 cups

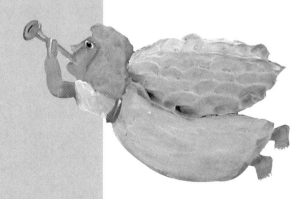

Breads

BREADS

SOUTHERN BISCUITS

2	cups all-purpose flour
4	teaspoons baking powder
1	teaspoon salt
1	teaspoon granulated sugar
½	cup margarine
1	egg in measuring cup with milk to equal ⅔ cup

Preheat oven to 425°. Combine dry ingredients. Add margarine and cut in until well blended and the mixture resembles meal. Add egg and milk. Stir into flour mixture until there are no dry particles. Turn out onto floured counter and work gently for a moment until dough looks smooth. (Do not over handle.) Roll out ½-inch thick. Cut with a biscuit cutter to desired size. Bake on a baking sheet for 8-10 minutes or until barely brown.

Cook's Note: *For cranberry orange scones, add ½ cup dried cranberries and 1 teaspoon grated orange rind to flour mixture before adding egg and milk. For currant scones, add ½ cup currants and 1 teaspoon grated lemon rind and follow directions above.*

Yield: 1 dozen 2-inch biscuits or 2 dozen 1-inch biscuits

> *My aunt was a wonderful cook. She made yeast rolls every day and they would rise and we would have fresh rolls every night. We would toast the leftovers in the morning, which was heaven.*

BLUE CHEESE BISCUITS

1	package regular size refrigerator dough biscuits (not grand)
3	tablespoons blue cheese, crumbled
½	cup butter

Preheat oven to 400°. Cut biscuits into quarters and place the wide side down in a greased 12-cup muffin tin. Melt together butter and blue cheese; pour mixture over biscuits. Bake for 10-15 minutes or until golden brown.

Cook's Note: *The better the blue cheese, the better the taste.*

Yield: 6-8 servings

WILLIAMSBURG SWEET POTATO BISCUITS

1½	cups all-purpose flour
2	tablespoons light brown sugar
4	teaspoons double-acting baking powder
1	teaspoon salt
½	teaspoon cinnamon
¼	teaspoon ground cloves
4	tablespoons butter, cut into bits
1	cup puréed cooked sweet potato
½	cup milk

Preheat oven to 425°. In a bowl sift together flour, brown sugar, baking powder, salt, cinnamon, and cloves. Add butter and combine the mixture until it resembles corn meal. Stir in puréed sweet potato and milk. Spoon the batter by heaping tablespoons onto a baking sheet and bake biscuits in the top third of a hot oven for 15 minutes.

Cook's Note: *The biscuits may be rolled out on a well-floured counter top if desired. They are wonderful for a different and yummy ham biscuit.*

Yield: 24 biscuits

CHEESE BISCUITS

½-¾	cup butter (½ for medium biscuits, ¾ for cocktail biscuits)
2	cups white self-rising flour
1	cup sour cream
2	cups grated Cheddar cheese

Preheat oven to 450°. Cut butter into flour until combined. Add sour cream and cheese and knead on a floured surface gently until combined. (Do not over handle). Roll out ¼-⅓-inches thick. Cut with a biscuit cutter to desired size. Bake on an ungreased baking sheet for 8-10 minutes.

Cook's Note: *Southern cooks prefer White Lily self-rising flour.*

Yield: 12 medium biscuits or 24 cocktail biscuits

TEX-MEX CORNSTICKS

1   cup yellow cornmeal
1   teaspoon granulated sugar
½   teaspoon baking soda
½   teaspoon salt
1   cup well-shaken buttermilk
1   large egg
4   ounces coarsely grated extra-sharp
    Cheddar cheese
¼   cup finely chopped scallion
    (white and pale green parts only)
1-2 tablespoons finely chopped, drained
    pickled jalapeño peppers
4   tablespoons unsalted butter, melted,
    divided

Preheat oven to 425°. Heat pans in middle of oven 10 minutes. Whisk together cornmeal, sugar, baking soda and salt in large bowl. Whisk together buttermilk and egg in another bowl; then add cornmeal mixture with Cheddar, scallion, jalapeño to taste, and 2 tablespoons butter stirring until just combined. Remove pans from oven and divide remaining 2 tablespoons butter among cornstick molds .Quickly divide batter among molds (about 3 tablespoons each) and bake 12-15 minutes until a tester comes out clean and tops are golden. Cool cornsticks in pans 3-5 minutes before removing from molds. Serve warm.

Cook's Note: *Special equipment: 2 well-seasoned cast-iron cornstick pans, each with 7 (5x1½-inch) molds or a well-seasoned 9-inch cast-iron skillet*

Yield: 14 cornsticks or one 9-inch loaf.

PARMESAN TWISTS

- 1 cup freshly grated Parmesan cheese
- 1 cup all-purpose flour
- 7 tablespoons sour cream
- ¼ cup butter
  Pinch of coarse salt
  Pinch of paprika

Place all ingredients in bowl of a food processor and mix until dough is well combined. Press dough into a flat disk and wrap in wax paper. Chill for 30 minutes. Preheat oven to 350°. On a lightly floured surface, roll the dough into a ¼-inch thick rectangle, about 12-inches wide and 9-inches long. Cut dough into strips about ½-inch wide. Twist each strip into a spiral twisting the ends and turning. Place the twists on an ungreased baking sheet and gently press the edges into the sheet to keep strip from untwisting. Bake for 15 minutes or until golden brown. Serve warm.

Cook's Note: *If dough is getting soft when pressed onto baking sheet, chill twists for 15 minutes before baking.*

Yield: 24 twists

MIDDLESEX BATTER BREAD

- 3 cups whole milk
- ¾ cup sifted cornmeal
- 3 large eggs, beaten
- 1 teaspoon salt
- 1 teaspoon baking powder
- 1 tablespoon butter

Preheat oven to 400°. Butter a 2-quart casserole and warm in oven while mixing bread, being careful not to let butter burn. Heat milk and add cornmeal gradually, stirring constantly. Add eggs, salt, baking powder, and butter, still stirring. Gently stir mixture until thickened. Transfer to casserole and bake for 30 minutes.

Yield: 6-8 servings

HERBED PITA TOASTS

¾ cup butter, softened
2 tablespoons minced parsley
1 tablespoon snipped chives
1 tablespoon fresh lemon juice
1 clove garlic, minced
  Salt and freshly ground pepper to taste
6 pita loaves, white or whole wheat

Preheat oven to 450°. Cream together butter, parsley, chives, lemon juice, garlic, salt, and pepper in a medium-sized bowl. Let mixture stand, covered, for at least 1 hour. Halve pita loaves horizontally and separate each half into 2 pieces. Spread the inside of each piece with some of the butter mixture. Arrange the pita on a baking sheet in one layer and bake in the top third of oven for 5 minutes or until lightly browned and crisp.

Yield: 24 toasts

WELCOME

TIDEWATER BISCUIT MUFFINS

2½ cups all-purpose flour
¼ cup granulated sugar
1½ tablespoons baking powder
¼ teaspoon salt
6 tablespoons unsalted butter, softened
1 cup cold milk

Preheat oven to 350°. In bowl, combine flour, sugar, baking powder and salt; mix well, breaking up any lumps. Work butter in by hand until mixture resembles coarse cornmeal, making sure no lumps are left. Gradually stir in milk, mixing just until dry ingredients are moistened. (Do not over beat). Spoon batter into 12 greased muffin cups. Bake 35-40 minutes until golden brown. The finished muffins should have a thick crust with cake-like center.

Yield: 1 dozen

GOLDEN RAISIN IRISH SODA BREAD

2	cups unbleached all-purpose flour plus additional for sprinkling
¼	cup wheat bran (not bran cereal) or toasted wheat germ
1	teaspoon baking soda
½	teaspoon salt
¼	cup cold, unsalted butter, cut into bits
1	cup golden raisins
1	cup buttermilk or plain yogurt

Preheat oven to 400° and sprinkle baking sheet lightly with flour. In large bowl, whisk flour, wheat germ, baking soda, and salt. Add butter and toss to coat with flour. With fingertips rub in butter until mixture resembles coarse meal. Add raisins and toss until coated. Add buttermilk or yogurt and stir until dough is moistened evenly. On a floured surface knead dough 1 minute, sprinkling lightly with additional flour to prevent sticking (dough should remain soft). Shape dough into a ball. On a greased baking sheet, pat dough out into a 6-inch round. Sprinkle round with additional flour and with fingertips spread lightly over round. With a sharp knife cut a shallow X in top of round. Bake bread in middle of oven 35-45 minutes, or until golden brown. Wrap bread in a kitchen towel and cool on rack 1 hour. Unwrap and cool 1 hour more.

Yield: 1 loaf

"LUCKY STARS"

LEMON TEA BREAD

6	tablespoons corn oil margarine
1½	cups granulated sugar, divided
2	eggs
½	cup whole milk
1½	cups all-purpose flour
1	teaspoon baking powder
⅛	teaspoon salt
½	cup chopped English walnuts
1	lemon, juiced and rind grated

Preheat oven to 350°. Cream margarine and 1 cup sugar; add eggs and beat well. Add milk, flour, baking powder and salt alternately to creamed mixture. Stir in nuts and lemon rind. Pour into a greased 9x5-inch loaf pan. Bake 50-55 minutes. Combine ½ cup sugar with lemon juice to use as a glaze. Remove bread from pan and spoon glaze over top immediately.

Cook's Note: *For gift-giving this recipe will make 4 miniature loaves. Bake miniature loaves approximately 30 minutes or until center springs back when touched lightly. Loaves can be frozen.*

Yield: 1 large loaf or 4 miniature loaves

CHOCOLATE CHIP BANANA BREAD

4	ripe bananas, mashed
½	cup granulated sugar
½	cup brown sugar
1	large egg, beaten
1½	cups all-purpose flour
½	cup butter, melted
1	teaspoon baking soda
	Dash salt
¾	cup semi-sweet chocolate chips

Preheat oven to 325°. Grease and flour a 9x5x2½-inch loaf pan. Mash bananas with a fork in a large bowl. Stir in remaining ingredients in the order listed. Pour into loaf pan and bake for 55 minutes or until done.

Cook's Note: *A great way to use over-ripe bananas. This is a yummy treat with coffee or as a snack.*

Yield: 1 loaf

CRANBERRY ORANGE BREAD

3   medium oranges
I   large egg, beaten
2   tablespoons cooking oil
2   cups all-purpose flour
¾   cup granulated sugar
I½   teaspoons baking powder
I   teaspoon salt
½   teaspoon baking soda
I   cup coarsely chopped fresh cranberries
½   cup chopped walnuts
I   cup sifted confectioners' sugar

Preheat oven to 350°. Squeeze all juice from oranges. Measure ¾ cup orange juice and reserve rest. In a mixing bowl, combine measured orange juice, egg and oil. In another mixing bowl, stir together flour, sugar, baking powder, salt, and baking soda. Add juice mixture to dry ingredients and stir just until moistened. Fold in chopped cranberries and walnuts. Turn batter into lightly greased 8x4x2-inch loaf pan or three 6x3x2-inch loaf pans. Bake 50-60 minutes for large pan or 30-40 minutes for smaller pans. Cool bread for 10 minutes, and remove from pan onto a wire rack to cool. For glaze, stir one tablespoon reserved orange juice into confectioners' sugar. Add more juice to make desired consistency. Drizzle glaze on top of cooled loaf.

Cook's Note: *If baking small loaves, treat your neighbors to a holiday gift wrapped in plastic wrap and tied with wired ribbon and holly leaves.*

Yield: I large loaf or 3 small loaves

YOGURT LOAF WITH MARMALADE GLAZE

1½ cups all-purpose flour
2   teaspoons baking powder
¼   teaspoon salt
1   cup plain whole-milk yogurt
1   cup granulated sugar
3   large eggs
1   teaspoon finely grated lemon peel, packed
¼   teaspoon vanilla extract
½   cup vegetable oil
¼   cup lemon, orange, or grapefruit
     marmalade
1   teaspoon water

Position rack in center of oven and preheat 350°. Generously butter 8½x4½x2½-inch metal loaf pan. Sift flour, baking powder, and salt into medium bowl. Combine yogurt, sugar, eggs, lemon peel, and vanilla in large bowl; whisk until well blended. Gradually whisk in dry ingredients. Using rubber spatula, fold in oil. Transfer batter to prepared pan and place pan on baking sheet. Place baking sheet with pan in oven and bake about 50 minutes until cake begins to pull away from sides of pan and tester inserted into center comes out clean. Cool cake in pan on rack 5 minutes. Cut around sides to loosen and turn cake out onto rack. Turn cake upright and cool completely. For glaze, stir marmalade and water in small saucepan over medium heat until marmalade melts. Brush hot mixture over top of cake and let cool. Cut into slices and serve.

Cook's Note: *Cake can be made 1 day ahead and wrapped to store at room temperature. Cake can be served for breakfast or with fresh fruit for dessert.*

Yield: 1 loaf or 8 servings

BLUEBERRY COFFEE CAKE

1	cup butter or margarine, softened
2	cups granulated sugar
4	eggs
1½	teaspoons vanilla extract
1	pint fresh blueberries, washed and well-drained
3	cups all-purpose flour, divided
1	teaspoon baking powder
½	teaspoon salt

Preheat oven to 325°. Grease and flour a 10-inch tube pan. Use mixer to cream butter and sugar. Add eggs one at a time, beating well after each addition. Add vanilla and beat until fluffy. Dredge berries with ¼ cup of flour and set aside. Sift remaining flour with baking powder and salt; fold into cake batter until well blended. Gently stir in berries. Pour into pan and bake for 50 minutes or until cake tester inserted near center comes out clean. Place pan on rack and cool in pan for 10 minutes before removing from pan.

Cook's Note: *16-ounce package frozen blueberries may be used.*
· *Travels well.*

Yield: 12-16 servings

For Christmas, all the kids would wait at the top of the stairs. Then we'd come down in a rush. We'd have the traditional breakfast with fresh coffee cake.

SUMMER

CARAMEL-PECAN COFFEE RING

1	(16-ounce) package hot roll mix
⅔	cup warm water, 105° to 115°
2	eggs, slightly beaten
6	tablespoons butter or margarine, melted and divided
½	cup firmly packed brown sugar
3	tablespoons butter or margarine, softened
3	tablespoons dark corn syrup
⅓	cup chopped pecans
¾	cup firmly packed brown sugar
1¼	teaspoons ground cinnamon
10	pecan halves

Remove yeast package from roll mix. Sprinkle yeast over warm water in large mixing bowl; let stand 5 minutes. Stir in eggs and 3 tablespoons melted butter. Add roll mix. Beat at low speed of an electric mixer until mixture forms soft dough. Place dough in large greased bowl, turning to grease top. Cover and let rise in a warm place (85°), free from drafts, 45 minutes or until doubled in bulk. Combine ½ cup brown sugar, softened butter, and corn syrup; beat at medium speed of electric mixer until well blended. Stir in chopped pecans. Set aside. Punch dough down. Turn out onto a floured surface. Knead 5 minutes. Roll dough to a 16x12-inch rectangle; spread with 3 tablespoons melted butter. Combine ¾ cup brown sugar and cinnamon; stir well. Sprinkle mixture over dough. Roll up dough, jellyroll fashion, starting at long side. Pinch seam to seal but not sealing ends. Cut roll into 16 one-inch slices; press a pecan half into the cut side of 10 slices. Grease a 10-inch tube pan. Spoon reserved brown sugar mixture into pan. Place 10 dough slices along outside edge of pan, allowing cut sides with pecans to stand against side of pan. Stand remaining 6 slices against inside of pan. Cover and let rise in a warm place, free from drafts, 45 minutes or until doubled in bulk. Bake at 325° for 30-35 minutes or until done. Let cool 2 minutes; invert coffee cake onto serving place. Serve immediately.

Yield: one 10-inch coffee cake

Food friendships? Marcel Desaulniers, Rowena Fullinwider, Sydney Mears... and Daniel May. He's just retired and he was the president of the International Association of Culinary Professionals, he's the one who's been very helpful to me. Called me to see if I would be involved in Julia Child's celebration. And he's called me to do awards for them to give out to the culinary professionals...the fork with the food on it? That was one of the awards.

WELSH RAREBIT

2	egg yolks
1	tablespoon Dijon mustard
¼	cup heavy cream
5	cups shredded Cheddar cheese
12	slices hearty bread
2	large tomatoes, sliced
1	small bunch watercress

Cream together egg yolks, mustard and cream. Add cheese and work into a spreadable paste. Place bread on a baking sheet and broil first side until brown. Spread mixture onto untoasted side of bread. Return to broiler until bubbling. Serve topped with tomatoes and watercress.

Yield: 6 servings

OPEN-FACE HAM, CHEDDAR, AND APPLE BUTTER SANDWICHES

3	ciabatta rolls, halved horizontally, or 6 thick slices country-style bread
2	tablespoons olive oil
6	tablespoons apple butter
4	tablespoons Dijon mustard
1¼	pounds Black Forest ham, thinly sliced
12	ounces extra-sharp white Cheddar cheese, sliced
1	bunch fresh chives, chopped

Brush cut side of ciabatta rolls with oil. Place rolls, cut side up, on baking sheet. Broil about 2 minutes until rolls begin to brown around edges. Spread apple butter and mustard on each roll half. Top with ham, then cheese. Broil about 2 minutes until cheese melts and begins to brown in spots. Sprinkle with chives and serve.

Cook's Note: *Thinly sliced roasted turkey may be substituted for ham.*

Yield: 6 servings

MEDITERRANEAN TUNA SANDWICHES

¼ cup olive oil
½ cup red wine vinegar
Grated Parmesan cheese
Black pepper
1 red onion, sliced very thinly
Fresh baguette or Kaiser rolls, sliced horizontally
1 (6-ounce) can tuna
Capers, drained and rinsed
Kalamata olives, sliced
1 tomato, sliced into eighths
Leafy greens, washed, dried and torn

In small bowl, whisk together olive oil, red wine vinegar, cheese, and pepper. Add onions to mixture and let marinate while preparing remaining ingredients. Hollow out bread a little to form pouch. Set out bottom slice of bread, drizzle thinly with oil-vinegar mixture and layer onions. Follow with tuna, capers, olives, leafy greens, and tomato. Drizzle lightly with oil-vinegar mixture and top with bread. Compress sandwich firmly and let sit for a few minutes before serving.

Yield: 4 servings

TAILGATE SANDWICHES

1	large red bell pepper, halved and seeded
1	French baguette or 6 small French rolls
1	tablespoon olive oil
1	tablespoon red wine vinegar
6	thin slices mozzarella cheese
6	leaves red or green leaf lettuce, washed, dried
6	thin slices ripe tomato
	Freshly ground black pepper
6	thin slices smoked turkey

Preheat broiler. Cover baking sheet with aluminum foil. Slightly flatten pepper halves and place under broiler until skin is charred black. Place in plastic bag and seal. After 10 minutes, remove skin and cut peppers lengthwise. Slice rolls or bread and brush with olive oil and vinegar. Layer cheese, lettuce, tomatoes, sprinkling of black pepper, red peppers, and turkey. Wrap tightly with plastic wrap and refrigerate. Let wrapped sandwich sit at room temperature 1 hour before serving.

Yield: 6 servings

AUTUMN

48

WILD MUSHROOM AND FONTINA SANDWICHES

1	pound mixed fresh shiitake, chanterelle, and porcini mushrooms
5	tablespoons olive oil
1	teaspoon minced fresh rosemary
	Salt and black pepper
2	medium shallots, minced
1	teaspoon minced fresh thyme
¼	cup Marsala wine
4	½-inch-thick center-cut slices country style sour dough bread
6	ounces Italian fontina cheese, coarsely grated
2	tablespoons minced fresh parsley

Stem shiitake mushrooms. Cut all mushrooms lengthwise into ½-inch thick slices. Heat olive oil in large nonstick skillet over medium-high heat. Add rosemary and stir 10 seconds, then add mushrooms. Sprinkle with salt and pepper. Sauté mushrooms about 10 minutes until they begin to brown. Add shallots and thyme, stir 2 minutes. Add Marsala and boil about 30 seconds until evaporated. Remove from heat. Adjust seasonings. (Can be prepared 1 hour ahead. Let stand at room temperature.)

Preheat broiler. Place bread slices on baking sheet; broil about 2 minutes per side until lightly toasted. Divide cheese among bread slices, covering completely. Broil about 2 minutes until cheese melts. Rewarm mushrooms over medium heat if necessary. Mix in parsley. Place toasts on plates and spoon mushrooms over and serve.

Yield: 4 servings

We were flying to Paris and this French man was coming down the aisle, carrying a cat in a cage that was making a huge noise, and everyone was complaining and I, like an idiot, said to the man, "We'll move over so you can sit on the aisle here." So he sat down, put the cat on the floor, and the cat started scratching my leg. I thought, "I can't believe this, I'll get cat scratch fever or something." So the man and I started talking. His name was Dennis and he lived in Paris and we started talking about food—always a nice common denominator. He said there was this little restaurant

PROSCIUTTO, MOZZARELLA, TOMATO, AND BASIL PANINI

½ cup olive oil
3 tablespoons balsamic vinegar
1 large clove garlic, minced
  Salt and black pepper
8 ounces thinly sliced prosciutto
10 ounces thinly sliced whole-milk mozzarella
  cheese
12 tomato slices
12 large fresh basil leaves
1 (16-ounce) loaf ciabatta bread,
  13x6½x1½-inches, halved horizontally

Whisk olive oil, vinegar, and garlic in small bowl to blend; season dressing to taste with salt and pepper. Layer prosciutto, mozzarella, tomatoes, and basil over bottom of bread. Drizzle lightly with dressing, and then sprinkle with salt and pepper. Press top of bread over. Cut bread equally into 4 sandwiches. Prepare sandwich grill or panini grill to medium heat. Grill sandwiches about 5 minutes per side until bread is golden brown and cheese melts, pressing occasionally to compact with large spatula.

Yield: 4 servings

right around the corner from where we were staying and he highly recommended it and he gave me his card for us to show to the owner. So that was the first place we went after we got settled in, and it was wonderful. We would never have found it in a million years. It was teeny tiny. We had Dennis' card and they laid out the red carpet for us. I love things where you think you're in a nightmare situation with a cat scratching your leg, and then something wonderful comes out of it.

GOAT CHEESE PITA PIZZA

1	pita, 6½-inch diameter
⅓	cup prepared marinara sauce
3	ounces fresh goat cheese, broken into large clumps
2	teaspoons fresh thyme leaves or ½ teaspoon dried
2	tablespoons finely slivered red onion
4	black olives, sliced diagonally
1	tablespoon finely diced red bell pepper
1	tablespoon extra-virgin olive oil
	Freshly ground black pepper, to taste
1	teaspoon freshly grated lemon zest
1	tablespoon chopped flat-leaf parsley, for garnish

Preheat oven to 450°. Place the pita on a baking sheet. Spread sauce to within ½-inch of edges; crumble cheese on top. Sprinkle with thyme, onions, olives, and peppers. Drizzle with olive oil. Season with pepper. Bake about 10 minutes until the cheese is melted. When pizza is removed from the oven, sprinkle with lemon zest and parsley.

Yield: 2 servings as appetizer or 1 as entrée

RADICCHIO, FONTINA, AND GOAT CHEESE PIZZA

1½ tablespoons olive oil
2 large cloves garlic, minced
3 cups ½-inch wide strips radicchio
1¼ cups grated fontina cheese
1 cup thinly sliced fennel (1 medium bulb)
½ cup sliced roasted red peppers
 Salt and black pepper
10 ounce baked pizza crust
⅔ cup goat cheese
 Parmesan cheese shavings

Position rack in center of oven and preheat to 425°. Mix olive oil and garlic. Add radicchio, fontina, fennel, and peppers. Sprinkle with salt and pepper. Place pizza on baking sheet. Mound mixture in middle of crust to within ¾ inches of the border. Top with goat cheese. Bake about 13 minutes. Top with Parmesan shavings before serving.

Yield: 2 servings

TOMATO AND YELLOW PEPPER PITA PIZZA

I	pita, 6½-inches diameter
⅓	cup prepared marinara sauce
⅓	cup diced fresh mozzarella cheese, ¼-inch pieces
4-6	grape tomatoes, halved
2-3	tablespoons thinly slivered red onion
½	yellow bell pepper, cut into ¼-inch slices
4-6	black olives, sliced diagonally
I	tablespoon finely slivered fresh basil leaves
I	tablespoon extra-virgin olive oil
	Freshly ground black pepper, to taste

Preheat oven to 450°. Place pita on baking sheet. Spread sauce to within ½-inch of edge. Sprinkle with mozzarella. Arrange tomato halves, onions, peppers, and olives decoratively over cheese. Sprinkle with basil, drizzle with olive oil, and season with pepper. Bake about 10 minutes until cheese is melted and the vegetables are tender. Remove to a serving plate. Serve whole, or cut into pieces.

Cook's Note: *Fresh mozzarella melts beautifully. It's one of the secrets to a great pizza!*

Yield: 2 servings as an appetizer and I as an entree

I've had restauranteurs commission me. Park Avenue Café in New York commissioned me to do all these pieces for the restaurant. I did this "Tattoo Lady" which was fabulous. She didn't work for him, but I did a lot of Uncle Sams for him that he loved. I love doing artwork for restaurants. I can be wilder. I love painting food and painting people in food situations. I can paint larger pieces, things people couldn't normally handle in their homes.

SMOKED GOUDA AND BALSAMIC ONION QUESADILLAS

2	tablespoons butter
1	large onion, thinly sliced
1	tablespoon golden brown sugar
1/4	teaspoon balsamic vinegar
1 1/2	cups grated smoked Gouda cheese
4	10-inch-diameter flour tortillas
2	ounces sliced prosciutto, chopped
2	tablespoons olive oil

Preheat oven to 350°. Melt butter in heavy medium skillet over low heat. Add onion, brown sugar, and vinegar; sauté until onion is golden brown, stirring frequently, about 25 minutes. Remove from heat. Cool to room temperature. Sprinkle cheese over half of each tortilla, dividing equally. Sprinkle prosciutto and caramelized onion over cheese. Fold other half of each tortilla over cheese mixture. Brush tortilla with olive oil. Transfer quesadillas to heavy large baking sheet. Bake until tortillas are golden and cheese melts, 5-10 minutes. Cut each into 6 triangles. Serve hot.

Yield: 4 servings for a "pizza" dinner or 6-8 as appetizer

CHICKEN JALAPEÑO JACK QUESADILLAS WITH MANGO SALSA

2	tablespoons vegetable oil
3	pounds chicken breasts, boneless, skinless
2	teaspoons salt, or to taste
1	teaspoon freshly ground black pepper, or to taste
4	mangoes, diced
1	papaya, diced
1	chipotle pepper, canned, minced
¼	cup orange juice
¼	cup lime juice
4	cups jalapeño-jack cheese, grated
6	scallions, thinly sliced
1	cup peanuts, toasted, roughly chopped
16	whole wheat flour tortillas
3	tablespoons peanut oil

Preheat oven to 400°. Heat vegetable oil over high heat in large sauté pan. Season chicken with salt and pepper. Cook chicken breasts until golden brown on all sides, about 8-10 minutes. Place chicken in oven until cooked through, about 10-12 minutes total. Allow the chicken to cool for 5 minutes. Shred chicken into bite-sized pieces. While chicken is cooking, combine mango, papaya, chipotle pepper, orange juice, and lime juice. Reserve the salsa under refrigeration until needed. To assemble quesadillas, place ¾ cup chicken, ½ cup jalapeño-jack cheese, ¾ cup scallions, and 2 tablespoons peanuts on tortilla. Top with another tortilla. Repeat with remaining ingredients to make 8 quesadillas. Heat about 1 teaspoon peanut oil in large sauté pan. Place 1 quesadilla in pan and lightly brown on both sides, making certain that the cheese is melted in the middle before removing from the heat. Repeat with remaining quesadillas, adding more peanut oil when necessary. Cut each quesadilla into fourths and serve with the mango salsa.

Cook's Note: *Rotisserie chicken may be used.*

Yield: 8 servings

Soups

NANCY THOMAS © 2006

SOUPS

ASPARAGUS SOUP WITH LEMON CREAM

3	pounds asparagus, tough ends removed
2	tablespoons butter
I	medium onion, coarsely chopped
6	cups chicken stock
2	tablespoons lemon juice, divided
	Salt and freshly ground white pepper
½	cup crème fraîche or yogurt
I	teaspoon grated lemon zest

Slice off 1-inch of the asparagus tips. Slice the tips diagonally into thin slivers and reserve. Cut the remaining asparagus into ¾-inch lengths. Melt butter in heavy saucepan over medium heat. Add onions and cook for 5 minutes. Add the asparagus and the stock. Bring to a boil over high heat. Reduce heat and simmer about 12 minutes until asparagus is tender. Let soup cool. Purée soup in batches in a blender until very smooth and light, 2-3 minutes per batch on high speed. Add 1 tablespoon of lemon juice and season to taste with salt and pepper. Add additional water if necessary to correct consistency if the soup is too thick. Add the thin pieces of asparagus tips to the soup and bring to a simmer over medium heat. Cook 2-3 minutes until tips are tender. If serving soup cold, cool in the refrigerator. If serving warm, keep covered over low heat. Meanwhile, in a small bowl mix together crème fraîche or yogurt, lemon zest, and remaining tablespoon of lemon juice. Add 1-2 tablespoons of water to thin slightly. This should be the consistency of barely whipped cream. Refrigerate until ready to use. To serve, ladle the soup into bowls and drizzle with lemon cream.

Yield: 6 serving

CREAM-LESS ASPARAGUS SOUP

SOUP

- 1 tablespoon olive oil
- 3 tablespoons diced leeks, white part only
- 2 tablespoons minced shallots
- 1 stalk celery, diced
- 1 medium carrot, peeled and diced
- 1 teaspoon garlic, minced
- 2 pounds asparagus, cut into 2-inch pieces, with tips removed and saved
- 6 cups chicken stock or vegetable broth
- 2 bay leaves, fresh preferred
- 1¼ teaspoons mustard seeds
- ¾ teaspoon salt
- ¼ teaspoon ground white pepper
- 2 medium Yukon Gold potatoes, peeled and roughly chopped
- 1 ounce sherry

GARNISH

- 1 tablespoon olive oil
- 8-10 shallots, peeled and cut in half
- Reserved asparagus tips

Heat oil in a saucepan over medium heat, and "sweat" the leeks, shallots, celery, carrot, and garlic for 3-4 minutes. Add the asparagus pieces, and cook for an additional 4-5 minutes, stirring occasionally. Add the chicken stock, bay leaves, mustard seeds, salt, pepper, and potatoes. Bring to a boil, reduce heat and simmer for about 20 minutes or until asparagus is tender. Remove bay leaves, and purée soup thoroughly in a blender. Strain purée and return to saucepan over low heat. Stir in sherry. To prepare garnish, heat olive oil in a sauté pan, and cook shallots until they begin to brown. Blanch asparagus tips in boiling water until crisp-tender. Top soup with shallots and asparagus tips and serve.

Yield: 6-8 servings

GINGERED CARROT SOUP WITH CHIVES AND CRÈME FRAÎCHE

1	tablespoon butter
½	cup chopped onion
2	cloves garlic, minced
5	cups peeled and thinly sliced carrots
1	tablespoon fresh minced ginger
4	cups chicken or vegetable stock
¼	cup freshly squeezed lime juice
	Freshly ground white pepper
1	cup crème fraîche or yogurt
¼	cup finely chopped fresh chives

In a medium saucepan, melt butter over medium low heat. Add onion and cook about 10 minutes, until soft. Add garlic and cook another 2-3 minutes. Stir in carrots and ginger. Add stock and simmer about 20 minutes, until carrots are tender. Add lime juice with a pinch of white pepper. Adjust seasoning to taste. Purée warm soup in a blender until smooth. Serve warm or cold topped with a spoonful of the crème fraîche or yogurt and a sprinkling of chives.

Yield: 4 servings

CURRIED ZUCCHINI SOUP

3	tablespoons butter
1	pound zucchini, sliced in ¼-inch rounds
1	large clove garlic, minced
¼	cup chopped shallots or scallions
1¼	cups chicken stock
¼	cup heavy cream
½	teaspoon curry
	Salt and white pepper to taste

In a sauté pan, melt butter; add zucchini, garlic and shallots. Cook over low heat until limp. Scrape into a food processor and blend. Add chicken stock; blend again. With processor running, add cream. Remove to storage container and stir in curry, salt and pepper. Chill 6 hours or overnight.

Yield: 4 servings

CREAMY MUSHROOM SOUP

1	medium carrot, chopped
½	medium onion, chopped
2	stalks celery, chopped
1	tablespoon oil
2	pounds cleaned button mushrooms
½	pound cleaned shiitake mushrooms
½	pound cleaned oyster mushrooms
1	tablespoon fresh chopped tarragon
1	teaspoon salt
1	teaspoon white pepper
3	pints chicken or vegetable stock
1	pint heavy cream
2	tablespoons melted butter or oil
2	tablespoons all-purpose flour

Mince carrots, onions, and celery in food processor and sauté in heavy pot with oil. Coarsely chop mushrooms in processor and add to pot with tarragon, salt, and pepper. Cook for about 15 minutes. Do not burn. Add stock and cream. Mix melted butter and flour until smooth and whip into soup. Bring to a boil, stirring constantly until all of the flour and butter mixture is incorporated and the soup is thickened. Simmer for 30 minutes and serve. Season to taste.

Yield: 8 servings

I get very emotional – like the Julia Child experience; that was wonderful. But I was really too excited to experience the food. I was so excited about the whole thing that the food became secondary. Now it's only when I'm very quiet and am eating someplace wonderful and can pay attention that I have wonderful food experiences. That can be embarrassing when you're dining with a chef and he asks you, how is the food? And I'm thinking, I don't have a clue, I'm just excited about being here!

POTATO-LEEK SOUP

3   medium-sized potatoes
3   cups leeks, cleaned, chopped
I   medium stalk celery, chopped
I   large carrot, chopped
4   cups water
I ½ teaspoons salt
I   cup milk
     Freshly ground black pepper
     Snippets of fresh herbs (thyme, marjoram,
       basil, chives), optional

Scrub potatoes and cut into 1-inch chunks. Place in a soup pot or Dutch oven with leeks, celery, carrot, water and salt. Bring to boil, cover, and cook about 20 minutes until the potatoes are tender. Remove from heat and let cool. Purée the soup in a blender or food processor in batches. Return purée to pot and stir in milk. Heat but do not boil; stirring frequently. Add pepper to taste and add salt if necessary. Serve hot or cold topped with a sprinkling of fresh herbs.

Cook's Note: *Equally delicious hot or cold, this thick, rich-tasting butter and oil free soup is very simple to make. Soymilk may be substituted for milk.*

Yield: 6 servings

ONION AND PORTABELLA SOUP WITH GOAT CHEESE CROUTONS

AUTUMN

3	tablespoons butter, divided
1½	pounds onions, halved, thinly sliced (about 5 cups)
4	fresh thyme sprigs
1½	pounds portabella mushrooms, stemmed, black gills removed, caps halved and cut crosswise into ¼-inch thick strips
3	tablespoons Cognac or brandy
2	cloves garlic, minced
8	cups canned vegetable broth
1	cup dry white wine
	Salt and freshly ground black pepper
18	(1-inch thick) slices French bread baguette, toasted
8	ounces soft fresh goat cheese, room temperature

Melt 1 tablespoon butter in heavy large pot over high heat. Add onions and thyme; sauté until onions begin to soften, about 8 minutes. Reduce heat to low; cook about 20 minutes until onions are caramelized, stirring occasionally. Transfer onion mixture to medium bowl. Melt remaining 2 tablespoons butter in same pot over medium high heat. Add mushrooms; sauté until soft, about 12 minutes. Add Cognac and garlic; stir 20 seconds. Stir in onion mixture, then broth and wine. Bring to boil. Reduce heat to low; simmer about 45 minutes until onions are very tender. Discard thyme sprigs. Season soup with salt and pepper. To prepare croutons, preheat broiler. Place baguette slices on large baking sheet. Spread goat cheese on slices, dividing equally. Broil goat cheese croutons until cheese begins to brown in spots, about 30 seconds. Divide soup among 6 bowls. Top with croutons and serve.

Cook's Note: *Can be made 1 day ahead. Cool slightly; cover and chill. Bring to simmer before serving.*

Yield: 6 servings

CREAM OF WATERCRESS SOUP

3	leeks, white parts, washed and chopped
1	small onion, chopped
2	tablespoons butter
3	medium-sized potatoes, peeled and chopped
3	cups chicken broth
1	cup milk
1	bunch watercress
	Salt and pepper to taste
1	cup heavy cream

Sauté leeks and onion in butter until golden. Add potatoes and stock. Cover and simmer 30 minutes. Cool. Purée in batches in blender. Pour mixture in saucepan and add milk. Cook 5 minutes and remove from heat. Cook watercress in ½ cup boiling water in a covered saucepan until it is limp. Cool. Purée in blender or finely chop and add to soup. Reheat. Add salt, pepper and cream. Repeat blending. Serve hot or cold.

Cook's Note: *Holds well in refrigerator and can be reheated in microwave.*

Yield: 4 servings

Most chefs don't expect anyone to have a developed palate except other chefs. They're just happy people like what they fix. I don't think it bothers them much… it's another experience.

BUTTERNUT SQUASH AND APPLE SOUP

1	small butternut squash (about 1 pound)
3	tart green apples
1	medium onion
¼	teaspoon dried rosemary
¼	teaspoon dried marjoram
3	(14½-ounce) cans chicken broth
2	cans water
2	slices white bread
	Salt and black pepper to taste
¼	cup heavy cream
2	tablespoons chopped parsley

Cut butternut squash in half, peel and seed. Peel, core and coarsely chop apples. Peel onion and chop coarsely. Combine these ingredients with rosemary, marjoram, chicken broth, water, bread, and salt and pepper in a heavy saucepan. Bring to a boil and simmer uncovered for 45 minutes. Cool. Purée soup in a blender until smooth, in several batches, not filling blender more than a quarter full each time. Return soup to saucepan and bring to a boil, then reduce heat. Just before serving, add heavy cream and serve hot with a sprinkle of fresh parsley on top.

Yield: 6 servings

SANTA FE CORN CHOWDER

6	medium ears of corn
6	strips of bacon, cut into ½-inch pieces
1	small onion, finely chopped
1	small green bell pepper, finely chopped
1	serrano or jalapeño pepper, seeded, deveined and chopped
1	small stalk celery, finely chopped
3	medium tomatoes, peeled, seeded, and finely chopped
2	medium boiling potatoes (about 1 pound), peeled and cubed
1	teaspoon salt
⅛	teaspoon ground allspice
	Pinch of granulated sugar
1	small bay leaf
2	cups light cream at room temperature
1	cup milk
	Freshly ground black pepper
	Cilantro or parsley, chopped, for garnish

Working over a bowl, cut the corn kernels from the cob at about half their depth. Then, using the back of the knife, scrape cobs over bowl to release all the "milk"; set aside. In a large non-reactive saucepan, fry bacon over moderately high heat about 10 minutes, stirring occasionally, until crisp. Transfer bacon to paper towels to drain. Crumble and reserve. Discard all but 3 tablespoons of bacon drippings from pan. Add onion and cook 4-5 minutes over moderate heat until golden. Add green bell pepper, jalapeño, and celery. Cook about 2 minutes until slightly softened. Add tomatoes, potatoes, salt, allspice, sugar, bay leaf, and the reserved corn kernels with their "milk". Stir well. Cook over moderate heat, stirring frequently, until the mixture begins to sizzle. Reduce heat to low. Cover and cook 35-45 minutes, stirring occasionally, until potatoes are tender. Stir in cream and milk and bring just to a boil. Remove from heat and season with black pepper to taste. Ladle the chowder into bowls and garnish with reserved crumbled bacon and cilantro or parsley.

Yield: 6 servings

CORN TOMATILLO SOUP

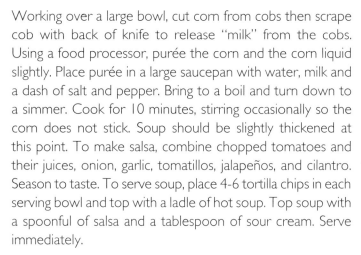

4	cups fresh corn (about 5 ears)
1	cup water
3½	cups milk
	Salt and freshly ground black pepper
2	pounds fresh tomatoes, chopped and juices reserved
1	large white onion, chopped
1	teaspoon minced garlic
4	tomatillos, blanched and chopped
1	jalapeño pepper, minced
4	tablespoons minced cilantro
½	cup sour cream
	Tortilla chips

Working over a large bowl, cut corn from cobs then scrape cob with back of knife to release "milk" from the cobs. Using a food processor, purée the corn and the corn liquid slightly. Place purée in a large saucepan with water, milk and a dash of salt and pepper. Bring to a boil and turn down to a simmer. Cook for 10 minutes, stirring occasionally so the corn does not stick. Soup should be slightly thickened at this point. To make salsa, combine chopped tomatoes and their juices, onion, garlic, tomatillos, jalapeños, and cilantro. Season to taste. To serve soup, place 4-6 tortilla chips in each serving bowl and top with a ladle of hot soup. Top soup with a spoonful of salsa and a tablespoon of sour cream. Serve immediately.

Cook's Note: *A very good prepared salsa may be purchased if you wish to save time.*

Yield: 4-6 servings

TUSCAN TOMATO SOUP WITH TORTELLINI

1	tablespoon plus 1 teaspoon olive oil
½	cup chopped onion
1	cup chopped carrot
½	cup chopped fennel, optional
2	cloves garlic, minced
1	teaspoon dried basil
1	teaspoon dried oregano
1	bay leaf
4	cups canned whole tomatoes in thick purée, chopped
2	cups water
2	cups chicken broth
1	(16-ounce) package dried cheese tortellini
2	cups escarole or spinach, shredded
	Italian parsley, chopped, for garnish

Heat olive oil in large stockpot; sauté onion, carrot, fennel, and garlic. Cook until vegetables are limp; stir in herbs and cook 1 minute. Stir in chopped tomatoes, 2 cups water, and chicken broth, and cook 15 minutes. Add pasta, and cook until tortellini is tender, adding additional water, if necessary. Add escarole or spinach, and cook 6 minutes. Garnish with parsley.

Cook's Note: *Dried cheese tortellini is in the pasta section of your food store and may be boxed or packaged.*

Yield: 8 servings

SPICY TOMATO SOUP

2	(32-ounce) cans whole tomatoes in juice, divided
1	large onion, coarsely chopped
1	teaspoon finely chopped garlic
1	teaspoon finely chopped fresh jalapeño pepper including seeds
2	teaspoons finely chopped, peeled fresh ginger
3	tablespoons olive oil
½	teaspoon ground cumin
2¼	cups reduced-sodium chicken broth
1	tablespoon granulated sugar or to taste
1	teaspoon salt or to taste

Drain 1 can tomatoes, discarding juice, then purée with remaining can tomatoes including juice in a blender. Cook onion, garlic, pepper, and ginger in oil in a 4-5 quart heavy nonreactive pot over moderate heat, stirring frequently, until onion is softened, about 8 minutes. Add cumin and cook, stirring 1 minute. Stir in puréed tomatoes, broth, sugar and salt and simmer, uncovered, stirring occasionally, 20 minutes. Working in batches, blend soup in blender until smooth. Transfer soup as blended to a sieve set over a large bowl and force through sieve, discarding seeds. Stir in additional sugar and salt to taste. Reheat in cleaned saucepan if necessary.

Yield: 4-6 servings

VEGETABLE SOUP WITH PISTOU

SOUP

- 3   quarts chicken stock
- 1½   pounds yellow-fleshed winter squash, peeled and cut into 1-inch cubes
- 2   cups shelled fresh white shell or cooked garbanzo beans

    Bouquet garni: parsley sprigs, bay leaf, thyme sprigs, and 1 piece dried orange peel, tied into a cheesecloth bag
- 2   potatoes, peeled and cut into chunks
- 2   yellow onions, thinly sliced
- 2   leeks, washed and sliced, including some tender green parts
- 1   cup coarsely chopped carrots
- 3   tomatoes, peeled, seeded, and coarsely chopped
- 4   ounces green beans, cut into 1-inch lengths
- 2   small zucchini, coarsely chopped

    Large handful of broken spaghetti or macaroni

PISTOU

     Large pinch of coarse salt
     Freshly ground black pepper to taste
- 4   large cloves garlic
     Large handful basil leaves
- ¼   cup freshly grated Parmesan cheese
- ¾   cup olive oil

It adds another dimension when you develop your palate. That's the thing. Of course, chefs are happy when you simply enjoy their food.

In a large kettle, heat chicken stock and add squash, beans, and bouquet garni. Cover and cook at a gentle boil for about 20 minutes. Add potatoes, onions, leeks, carrots, and tomatoes. Cover and cook 30 minutes longer. Add green beans, zucchini, and pasta. Cover and cook about 15 minutes more. While soup is cooking make pistou. Put salt, pepper, garlic, and basil in a food processor and pulse until all are reduced to a liquid paste. Add some cheese and mix until a stiff paste. Dribble in some olive oil, stirring until it becomes liquid again. Continue alternately adding cheese and olive oil until desired consistency. Remove bouquet garni from the soup and ladle hot soup into heated bowls. Serve with the pistou alongside.

Yield: 6-8 servings

68

LAURA'S "MEAN" GAZPACHO

GAZPACHO

2	cloves garlic, minced
1	teaspoon salt
1	(48-ounce) can tomato juice, (tomato-vegetable juice preferred)
2	teaspoons black pepper
2	tablespoons extra virgin olive oil
1	tablespoon red wine vinegar or red wine Zest and juice of one lemon
2	teaspoons Worcestershire sauce, optional
1	teaspoon hot pepper sauce, optional
2	large tomatoes, peeled, seeded
1	hothouse cucumber, peeled and seeded
1	sweet yellow or green bell pepper
3-4	scallions, thinly sliced
1	tablespoon chopped parsley
1½	teaspoons oregano
	Sour cream for garnish

PARMESAN CHEESE CROUTONS

2	cups French bread, cubed into 1-inch pieces
¼	cup olive oil
1	teaspoon salt
1	clove garlic, minced
1	teaspoon black pepper
¼	cup grated Parmesan cheese

SUMMER.

Mince garlic cloves with salt to make a paste. In a large bowl combine tomato juice with pepper, garlic paste, olive oil, vinegar, and lemon. Add Worcestershire and hot sauce if desired for added flavor. Chop tomatoes, cucumber, and bell pepper into ¼-inch pieces. Add to tomato juice mixture along with chopped scallions, parsley and oregano. Chill. For cheese croutons, toss all ingredients together by hand in a large bowl. Spread in a single layer on cookie sheet and bake in a 400° oven for 12 minutes or until golden brown. Midway, toss croutons once with spatula, to cook evenly. Watch carefully as croutons burn easily. Serve gazpacho chilled, garnished with sour cream and Parmesan croutons.

Yield: 10 servings

KALE AND WHITE BEAN SOUP

1	pound dried Great Northern beans
1	large onion, coarsely chopped
2	tablespoons olive oil
3	cloves garlic, finely chopped
5	cups chicken or vegetable broth
2	quarts water, divided
1	piece Parmigiano-Reggiano rind (2x3-inches)
2	teaspoons salt
1	teaspoon white pepper
1	bay leaf
1	teaspoon finely chopped fresh rosemary
1	pound smoked sausage (optional) sliced crosswise ¼-inch thick
8	carrots, halved lengthwise and cut crosswise into ½-inch pieces
1	pound kale, stems and center ribs discarded and leaves coarsely chopped

Cover beans with water, by 2 inches, in a pot and bring to a boil. Remove from heat and let stand, uncovered, 1 hour. Drain beans in a colander and rinse. Cook onions in oil in an 8-quart pot over moderately low heat, stirring occasionally, until softened, 4-5 minutes. Add garlic and cook, stirring, 1 minute. Add beans, broth, 1 quart water, cheese rind, salt, pepper, bay leaf, and rosemary and simmer, uncovered, until beans are just tender, about 50 minutes. While soup is simmering, brown sausage in batches in a heavy skillet over moderate heat, turning, then transfer to paper towels to drain. Stir carrots into soup and simmer 5 minutes. Stir in kale, sausage, and remaining quart water and simmer uncovered, stirring occasionally, until kale is tender, 12-15 minutes. Season soup with salt and pepper to taste.

Cook's Note: *Soup is best if made 1 or 2 days ahead and cooled completely, uncovered, then chilled, covered. Thin with water if necessary.*

Yield: 6-8 servings

WHITE BEAN SOUP WITH SMITHFIELD HAM AND WHITE CHEDDAR

4	tablespoons olive oil
1	cup diced carrots
1	cup diced celery
1½	cups diced onion
	Ham bone or ham trimmings
1	cup white wine
4	quarts chicken stock
	Cheese cloth bag tied with 5 sprigs thyme, 1 bay leaf, 1 tablespoon white peppercorns
8	cups cooked and drained Great Northern beans
3-4	cups 2% milk
	Salt and black pepper to taste
1	ounce white Cheddar cheese, diced
1	ounce Smithfield ham, sliced very thinly

In an 8-quart heavy-bottomed pot, in olive oil, cook carrots, celery, and onion with ham scraps until tender and without coloring. Add white wine and reduce by ⅔. Add chicken stock and the sachet and bring to a simmer and skim fat and impurities that rise to the top. Cook beans according to package directions. Add beans and simmer for 30-45 minutes. Remove the sachet and any ham bone and blend the soup in a blender until smooth. Bring back to a simmer; add milk until desired consistency is achieved. Season with salt and pepper. To serve, place 1 ounce of diced white Cheddar cheese and 1 ounce sliced Smithfield ham in the bottom of the bowls. Ladle the hot soup over and serve.

Yield: 10 servings

LENTIL SOUP

1	pound French green lentils
4	cups chopped yellow onions
4	cups chopped leeks, white part only
1	tablespoon minced garlic
¼	cup olive oil
1	teaspoon salt
1½	teaspoons freshly ground black pepper
1	tablespoon minced fresh thyme leaves
1	teaspoon ground cumin
3	cups medium-diced celery
3	cups medium-diced carrots
3	quarts chicken stock
1	(6-ounce) can tomato paste
2	tablespoons red wine vinegar
1	tablespoon olive oil
	Freshly grated Romano cheese

In a large bowl, cover lentils with boiling water and allow to sit for 15 minutes. Drain. In an 8-quart stockpot, sauté onions, leeks, and garlic with olive oil, salt, pepper, thyme, and cumin on medium heat for 20 minutes, until vegetables are translucent and very tender. Add celery and carrots and sauté for 10 more minutes. Add chicken stock, tomato paste, and lentils. Bring to a boil. Reduce heat and simmer uncovered for one hour, until lentils are cooked through. Adjust seasonings. Add red wine vinegar and serve hot, drizzled with olive oil and sprinkled with grated Romano.

Cook's Note: *Freezes well.*

Yield: 10-12 servings

TEXAS TORTILLA SOUP

SOUP

8	plum tomatoes
4	tablespoons olive oil, divided
1	medium-sized yellow onion, diced
1	red bell pepper, diced
6	cloves garlic, minced
2	teaspoons chili powder
2	teaspoons ground cumin
4	cups chicken stock
1	dried ancho chile pepper
1	(15-ounce) can peeled tomatoes
	Salt and freshly ground black pepper
3	chicken breasts, cooked and shredded
3	ears fresh corn or one 8-ounce package frozen corn, optional

GARNISHES

2	ripe avocados, peeled and sliced
	Tortilla chips or strips
2	plum tomatoes, diced
1/4	cup chopped fresh cilantro
1	cup shredded Monterey Jack cheese
	Sour cream, optional

Preheat oven to 350°. Slice tomatoes in half. Spread 1 tablespoon of olive oil on baking sheet and place tomatoes skin side up on sheet. Drizzle with another tablespoon of oil. Roast tomatoes for 25-30 minutes until tomatoes are slightly brown around edges and skins wrinkle. Heat remaining oil in heavy-bottomed 4-quart pot over medium heat. Add onion, bell pepper, and garlic and sauté 5 minutes or until vegetables become soft. Stir in chili powder and cumin and cook 1 minute. Add chicken stock and ancho chile. Bring to boil over medium-high heat, cover, decrease heat and simmer 15 minutes until chile softens. Remove chile from soup and discard stem. Cut chile in half and discard seeds if desired. Seeds make for spicier soup. Place softened chile, canned tomatoes with their juices, roasted tomatoes with their juices and any browned tomato bits in bowl of food processor. Purée mixture about 1 minute. Transfer mixture to the soup and continue simmering, covered, about 1 hour. Add salt and pepper to taste along with cooked chicken. If using fresh corn, cut kernels from the cobs and add to soup. Simmer for 5 minutes. Ladle soup into medium bowls and lean 3-4 slices of avocado against edge of each bowl. Arrange tortilla chips or strips in a similar way. Sprinkle each bowl with a handful of diced tomatoes, cilantro and shredded cheese. Top with sour cream.

Yield: 4-6 servings

PICANTE TACO SOUP

1	pound ground beef
1	medium onion, chopped
2	cloves garlic, minced
2	(14½-ounce) cans beef broth
1	(14½-ounce) can diced tomatoes, undrained
1½	cups picante sauce
1	cup uncooked spiral or small shell pasta
1	medium green bell pepper, chopped
2	teaspoons chili powder
1	teaspoon dried parsley flakes
	Shredded Cheddar cheese and tortilla chips for garnish

In a large saucepan, cook beef, onion, and garlic until meat is no longer pink; drain. Add the broth, tomatoes, picante sauce, pasta, green pepper, chili powder and parsley. Bring to a boil, stirring occasionally. Reduce heat; cover and simmer for 10-15 minutes or until pasta is tender. Garnish with cheese and tortilla chips.

Yield: 8 servings

SPICY SAUSAGE SOUP

1	pound spicy Italian sausage
1	Spanish onion, chopped
2	cloves garlic, minced
5	carrots, quartered lengthwise and chopped
5	stalks celery, quartered lengthwise and chopped
½	head Savoy cabbage, cored and chopped
1	(28-ounce) can whole tomatoes, drained and chopped
2	red new potatoes, cubed and cooked slightly (about 2 cups)
7-8	cups chicken broth
1	cup frozen or fresh green peas
	Kosher salt and black pepper to taste
¼	cup chopped fresh parsley
	Parmesan cheese, grated

Remove casing from sausage and crumble. Heat a large stockpot over medium high heat. Add sausage and cook until fat begins to render. Discard excess fat. Add onion, garlic, carrots, and celery, stirring well after each addition. Cook for 5 minutes. Add cabbage and cook, stirring occasionally, until limp and golden, about 15 minutes. Add tomatoes, potatoes, and chicken broth and bring to a boil. Reduce heat to low and cook for about 20 minutes. Add peas and cook 5 minutes. Add salt and pepper to taste. Serve with chopped parsley and grated Parmesan cheese.

Cook's Note: *May be frozen.*

Yield: 10-12 servings

KISS THE COOK

SPICY TURKEY CHILI

- 2-3 ancho or Poblano chile peppers
- 1 tablespoon ground cumin
- 2 cups chicken stock
- 1-2 canned Chipotle chiles in adobo sauce
- ¼ cup olive oil
- 1 cup chopped onion
- 2 tablespoons minced garlic
- 1½ pounds ground turkey
- 1 tablespoon dried oregano
- 2 teaspoons dried coriander
- Coarse salt and freshly ground black pepper
- 3 (15-ounce) cans pinto, Great Northern, kidney, or black beans or combination, drained and rinsed
- 1 (15-ounce) can diced tomatoes
- 8 corn tortillas, cut into 1-inch wide strips

In a skillet over medium heat toast ancho or Poblano chiles until they just begin to blacken about 2 minutes. Turn frequently. Remove from skillet. Tear the toasted chiles into pieces, discarding the stems, and place in a blender. Add chicken stock and Chipotle chiles and purée until smooth. Heat oil in a large pot over medium heat. Add onion and garlic and cook, stirring until translucent, about 3 minutes. Add turkey and cook, breaking meat into small pieces with a spoon, until meat is no longer pink, about 5 minutes. Stir in oregano, coriander and cumin. Season with salt and pepper and cook 5 minutes more. Add beans, tomatoes, and ancho purée to pot and stir to combine. Bring mixture to a boil and reduce to simmer. Cook partially covered until liquid has reduced and chili has thickened, 40-50 minutes. While chili is cooking, heat oven to 375°. Spread tortilla strips in a single layer on one or two baking sheets. Bake until crisp and just beginning to brown, 5-10 minutes. Remove from oven and cool. Serve chili warm with tortilla strips.

Cook's Note: *Optional additional garnishes are sour cream, diced red or green onion, fresh cilantro, or grated Monterey Jack cheese.*

Yield: 8 servings

SHRIMP BISQUE

1	pound uncooked shrimp, shelled and deveined
6	tablespoons butter
2	tablespoons grated onion
1	quart half-and-half
2	fish seasoning cubes
1	tablespoon white wine vinegar
2	tablespoons minced parsley or chives
¼	teaspoon salt
⅛	teaspoon freshly ground black pepper
⅛	teaspoon nutmeg, optional

Mince uncooked shrimp and set aside. Place butter in heavy pot; add onion and cook on low until onion is golden. Add half-and-half, fish seasoning cubes, and uncooked shrimp. Cook on low for 15-20 minutes. DO NOT BOIL! When ready to serve, stir in wine vinegar, parsley or chives, salt, pepper, and nutmeg.

Cook's Note: *This bisque is best made ahead of time and allowed to sit for at least 30 minutes to a day ahead before serving. Do not add last five ingredients until ready to serve.*

Yield: 6 servings

CHESAPEAKE BAY CRAB BISQUE

4	tablespoons butter, melted
1	small yellow onion, finely chopped
3	tablespoons all-purpose flour
2	cups light cream
2	cups whole milk
1	pound backfin crabmeat
2	tablespoons Sherry
	Salt and cayenne pepper to taste

Sauté onion in butter until translucent. Stir in flour. Add cream and milk, stirring constantly to make a roux. Simmer 5 minutes. Add crabmeat, Sherry, and seasonings. Heat thoroughly. Serve immediately.

Yield: 4 servings

CHESAPEAKE OYSTER BISQUE

1	pint oysters
1	chicken bouillon cube
1	teaspoon grated onion
1	large sprig parsley
1	bay leaf
3	tablespoons butter
4	tablespoons all-purpose flour
1	quart half-and-half
¾	teaspoon salt
	Dash white pepper
½	pint heavy cream

Chop oysters fine to release flavor. Pour oysters and liquor in a saucepan. Add bouillon cube, onion, parsley, and bay leaf. Cook gently for 3 minutes. Melt butter in top of large double boiler; add flour and stir until blended. Add half-and-half gradually and cook until somewhat thickened, stirring constantly. Add oyster mixture, salt, and pepper; stir in heavy cream. Reheat and serve after removing parsley and bay leaf.

Cook's Note: *Bisque may be made a day ahead.*

Yield: 4-6 servings

There was a place in New York called Blue Water Grill where they had an oyster tower... all the way down, on each level, different wines went with different oysters. It was heaven. To blend the wine with the oysters was just a remarkable experience. I couldn't have appreciated that twenty years ago.

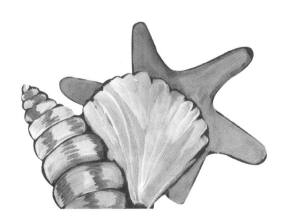

CAJUN CRABMEAT BISQUE

¾ cup butter
¾ cup all-purpose flour
3 tablespoons tomato paste
1½ cups finely chopped yellow onions
1 cup finely chopped celery
½ cup finely chopped scallions
4 cloves garlic, pressed
⅔ cup finely chopped green pepper
3 tablespoons finely chopped fresh parsley
2 quarts chicken stock
1 tablespoon Worcestershire sauce
1 bay leaf
1 teaspoon dried thyme
1 teaspoon salt
⅛ teaspoon black pepper
⅛ teaspoon cayenne pepper
½ teaspoon catsup
1 pound crabmeat

In a large heavy pot, melt butter and gradually add flour, stirring constantly until roux is golden brown, 20-30 minutes. Add tomato paste, onions, celery, scallions, garlic, and green pepper, cooking until tender. Add parsley and slowly stir in stock. Add Worcestershire, bay leaf, thyme, salt, black and cayenne pepper, and catsup. Add crabmeat. Cover and simmer 40 minutes, stirring occasionally.

Cook's Note: *This freezes beautifully.*

Yield: 8 servings

Salads

NANCY THOMAS 2002

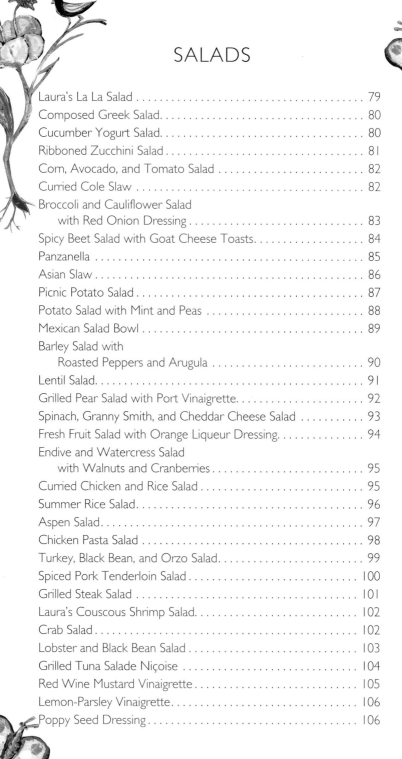

SALADS

LAURA'S LA LA SALAD

1	cup fresh green beans
1	cup fresh corn (about 1-2 cobs)
1	tablespoon fresh basil
2	teaspoons Dijon mustard
1	teaspoon salt
1	teaspoon black pepper
1	tablespoon balsamic vinegar
2	tablespoons extra-virgin olive oil
1	large tomato, diced
1	(10-ounce) can chickpeas, drained and rinsed
1	(10-ounce) can black olives, drained and sliced

Cook green beans to just crisp-tender, about 15 minutes in boiling water. Cool completely; cut into bite-size pieces. Break corncobs in half; cook in boiling salted water for about 10 minutes. Cool completely and cut kernels off, breaking kernels apart with fingers. (Beans and corn may be cooked in same boiling water.) To cool just cooked beans and corn quickly, place them in ice water for a few minutes, and then drain. Roll up basil leaves and slice into thin "ribbons". Whisk together mustard, salt, pepper, vinegar, and oil. Combine tomatoes, chickpeas, olives, corn, and green beans. Add basil and vinegar mixture. Toss well and serve chilled.

Yield: 6 servings

My daughter Laura, who went to Johnson & Wales, would look in my refrigerator, that I thought was empty, and my cupboard that was bare, and she would put these things together that I would never think of. And they were all delicious. Olives, couscous, and salsa, little combinations, and everything was fabulous. I was amazed at what she could find and put together, so I'd eat very well when she was here.

There's such a difference, I've noticed, in people who paint, but it's more about technique than about passion, and there's a huge difference. You can see it, feel it. And that's where I think it comes through you. That it's what's happening to you and you're doing it, rather than you're trying to paint something specific and you're thinking about it. People pick that up.

COMPOSED GREEK SALAD

1	(8-ounce) jar marinated artichoke hearts
2	large cucumbers, peeled, halved lengthwise, seeded, sliced crosswise
2	large tomatoes, cut into wedges
1	yellow bell pepper, sliced into rings
1	sweet onion, sliced into rings
20	Kalamata olives
10	tablespoons extra-virgin olive oil
4½	tablespoons white or red wine vinegar
1	tablespoon dried oregano
2	teaspoons grated lemon peel
1	cup crumbled feta cheese

Arrange artichokes, cucumbers, tomatoes, bell pepper, onion, and olives on large platter. Whisk oil, vinegar, oregano, and lemon peel in small bowl to blend. Season dressing to taste with salt and pepper. Pour dressing evenly over salad, sprinkle with feta cheese, and serve.

Yield: 8 to 10 servings

CUCUMBER YOGURT SALAD

3	hothouse cucumbers
1	tablespoon salt
1	cup plain yogurt
¼	cup snipped dill
2	tablespoons white wine vinegar
	Salt and freshly ground black pepper

Halve cucumbers lengthwise and, with a vegetable peeler or mandoline, shred halves into thin ribbons or strips. In a colander, toss cucumbers with salt and let drain for 20 minutes. In a bowl, combine yogurt, dill and vinegar. Add cucumbers, tossing mixture well. Season with salt and black pepper. Transfer to a salad bowl.

Yield: 6 servings

RIBBONED ZUCCHINI SALAD

2   pounds small zucchini, trimmed
1   teaspoon salt
2   tablespoons extra-virgin olive oil
2   teaspoons finely grated fresh lemon zest
2   teaspoons fresh lemon juice
2   teaspoons Dijon mustard
¼   teaspoon black pepper
3   ounces frisée, trimmed and torn into small pieces
½   cup loosely packed fresh flat-leaf parsley leaves
½   cup loosely packed fresh mint leaves, torn in half lengthwise if large
½   cup loosely packed fresh basil leaves, torn into small pieces
12 Kalamata or other brine-cured black olives, pitted and thinly sliced
1   small red onion, halved lengthwise and thinly sliced crosswise

Cut zucchini lengthwise with slicer into ⅛-inch-thick slices and transfer to a colander set over a bowl. Sprinkle zucchini with salt and toss to coat. Let stand 5 minutes, then rinse under cold water. Transfer zucchini to a clean kitchen towel and spread in 1 layer, then gently roll up towel to absorb excess water and let stand 5 minutes more. Whisk together oil, zest, juice, mustard, and pepper in a large bowl. Add zucchini, frisée, herbs, olives, and onion and toss to coat. Serve immediately.

Yield: 6 servings

CORN, AVOCADO, AND TOMATO SALAD

2	cups corn, cooked
1	avocado, diced
1	pint cherry or grape tomatoes, halved
½	cup finely chopped red onion
2	tablespoons olive oil
1	tablespoon fresh lime juice
½	teaspoon lime zest
¼	cup chopped cilantro, optional
¼	teaspoon salt
⅛	teaspoon freshly ground black pepper

Place corn in a large bowl, add avocado, tomatoes and onions. In a separate bowl, whisk together olive oil and remaining ingredients. Pour vinaigrette over salad and serve.

Yield: 4-6 servings

CURRIED COLE SLAW

1	small head cabbage or half a larger head
2	large carrots, peeled
⅓	cup mayonnaise
3	tablespoons cider vinegar
1	tablespoon granulated sugar
1	teaspoon salt
2	teaspoons poppy seeds
¼	teaspoon hot pepper sauce
1½	teaspoons curry powder

Trim cabbage and shred on a slicer, in a food processor, or by cutting it into thin slices with a sharp knife, yielding about 5 to 6 lightly packed cups of cabbage. Shred the carrots, yielding about 1 lightly packed cup. In a large bowl, whisk together mayonnaise, vinegar, sugar, salt, poppy seeds, hot pepper sauce, and curry powder. Add cabbage and carrots, mixing well. Serve immediately or cover, refrigerate and serve later. The cole slaw will keep, refrigerated, for 2 days.

Cook's Note: *The combination of curry and slaw is tangy and a perfect accompaniment for fish.*

Yield: 4-6 servings

BROCCOLI AND CAULIFLOWER SALAD WITH RED ONION DRESSING

½	cup olive oil
1	teaspoon dried crushed red pepper
¼	cup red wine vinegar
2	large garlic cloves, minced
2	cups thinly sliced red onions
6	cups broccoli florets
6	cups cauliflower florets
	Salt and black pepper

Heat oil and crushed red pepper in heavy small saucepan over medium-high heat about 1 minute, until oil begins to bubble around edge of pan. Pour into large bowl; cool to lukewarm. Whisk in vinegar and garlic. Mix onions into dressing. Let marinate at least 1 hour and up to 3 hours, tossing often. Cook broccoli and cauliflower florets in large pot of boiling salted water about 5 minutes until just crisp-tender. Drain; transfer to bowl of ice water to chill quickly. Drain very well and pat dry. Mix broccoli and cauliflower into dressing. Season with salt and pepper to taste. Let stand up to 1 hour, tossing occasionally. Serve at room temperature.

Cook's Note: *An unusual blend of flavors very good with grilled meat or poultry.*

Yield: 6 servings

84

SPICY BEET SALAD WITH GOAT CHEESE TOASTS

8	medium beets, greens removed and beets scrubbed
1	cup pure maple syrup
1	teaspoon cayenne pepper
2	tablespoons red wine vinegar
2	tablespoons extra virgin olive oil
1	teaspoon minced garlic
	Coarse salt and freshly ground black pepper
12	(¼-inch thick) baguette slices, toasted
4	ounces fresh goat cheese
1	teaspoon poppy seeds
12	ounces mesclun mix

In a medium saucepan, cover beets with water and bring to a boil. Simmer over medium heat, about 25 minutes, until just tender. Transfer beets to a plate and let cool; peel, and cut into ½-inch dice. Reserve 2 cups of the cooking liquid in the saucepan. Add maple syrup to saucepan and boil over medium high heat for 5 minutes. Stir in beets and cayenne and simmer over medium heat about 30 minutes until beets are sweet and hot. Using a slotted spoon, transfer beets to a plate. Boil cooking liquid about 8 minutes until slightly thickened. Return beets to pan and let cool to room temperature. In a small bowl, whisk 2 tablespoons of beet syrup with vinegar, olive oil, garlic, and salt. Spread each toast with 2 teaspoons of goat cheese and sprinkle with poppy seeds. In a large bowl, toss greens with the beets and just enough vinaigrette to coat everything lightly. Mound salad on plates and set goat cheese toasts on side.

Yield: 4 servings

There are wines that go with everything. The hardest one to find—and there is one—is a wine that goes with the vinegar in a salad.

PANZANELLA

SALAD

3	tablespoons extra virgin olive oil
1	small French bread or baguette, cut into 1-inch cubes
1	teaspoon Kosher salt
2	large ripe tomatoes, cut into 1-inch cubes
1	hothouse cucumber, sliced ½-inch thick
1	red bell pepper, seeded and cut into 1-inch cubes
1	yellow bell pepper, seeded and cut into 1-inch cubes
½	red onion, cut in half and thinly sliced
20	large basil leaves, coarsely chopped
2	tablespoons capers, drained
	Salt and black pepper

VINAIGRETTE

1	teaspoon finely minced garlic
½	teaspoon Dijon mustard
3	tablespoons Sherry or red wine vinegar
½	cup extra virgin olive oil
½	teaspoon Kosher salt
¼	teaspoon freshly ground black pepper

Heat oil in large sauté pan. Add bread and salt; cook over low to medium heat, tossing frequently, for 10 minutes, or until nicely browned. Add more oil as needed. For the vinaigrette, whisk together ingredients. In a large bowl, mix tomatoes, cucumber, red pepper, yellow pepper, red onion, basil, and capers. Add bread cubes and toss with vinaigrette. Season with salt and pepper. Serve, or allow salad to sit for about half an hour for flavors to blend.

Cook's Note: *A bright Italian bowl is a must for serving this colorful, refreshing salad.*

Yield: 12 servings

ASIAN SLAW

I don't entertain as much as I used to, but one of my favorite combinations is—I like contrasts— is my red ware with fancy silverware. Then I like to use hand-blown green glasses. All on white linen...

I love to set a table and have little salts.

I love making little arrangements, like running around the garden and cutting some pyracantha.

For myself, I like small arrangements by the bed or wherever my eye would hit. For my shows, I like the big dramatic arrangements.

DRESSING
3	tablespoons oil
3	tablespoons peanut butter
¼	cup rice vinegar
2	tablespoons soy sauce
I	teaspoon grated gingerroot
⅛	teaspoon crushed red pepper flakes

SALAD
2	cups thinly sliced Chinese (napa) cabbage
I	cup thinly sliced red cabbage
4	ounces fresh snow pea pods, trimmed, cut in half diagonally
I	cup fresh baby carrots, quartered lengthwise
I	small red bell pepper, cut into thin strips
I	(3 or 3.5-ounce) package any flavor ramen noodle soup mix
¼	cup dry-roasted peanuts, coarsely chopped

In a medium nonmetal bowl, combine oil and peanut butter; mix with wire whisk until well blended. Add all remaining dressing ingredients; blend well. In a large bowl, combine all salad ingredients except soup mix and peanuts; toss to mix. Discard seasoning packet from soup mix or reserve for another use. Crumble noodles; add to cabbage mixture. Add dressing and peanuts; toss to coat.

Yield: 4 servings

PICNIC POTATO SALAD

2½ pounds small red potatoes
    Salt
1   tablespoon lemon juice
½   cup sour cream
½   cup mayonnaise
¼   cup fresh basil cut into strips
¼   cup fresh parsley, minced
1   medium clove garlic, minced
2   tablespoons apple cider vinegar
1   teaspoon Worcestershire sauce
½   teaspoon Dijon mustard
¼   teaspoon freshly ground black pepper
½   teaspoon salt

Cover potatoes with lightly salted water and add lemon juice. Bring to a rapid boil and turn down heat to a rolling boil. Cook potatoes 12 minutes or until tender when pierced with a knife. Whisk together all other ingredients. Cut cooled potatoes into large chunks and toss with dressing. Refrigerate until time to serve.

Cook's Note: *Serve as a side dish in a green pottery cabbage bowl in the summer with grilled chicken.*

Yield: 6-8 servings

the CENTRE of Attraction

88

POTATO SALAD WITH MINT AND PEAS

2	pounds small red potatoes
	Salt
2	tablespoons white wine vinegar
1	tablespoon minced shallot
1	teaspoon salt
½	teaspoon black pepper
3	tablespoons extra-virgin olive oil
1	cup thawed frozen or cooked fresh baby peas
⅓	cup chopped or torn fresh mint leaves

Cover potatoes with cold salted water in a 3-quart saucepan, simmer, covered until tender, 10-15 minutes. While potatoes cook, whisk together vinegar, shallot, salt, and pepper in a large serving bowl. Drain potatoes and halve or quarter if desired. Add to vinegar mixture while warm and toss to coat. Add oil, peas, and mint and toss to combine. Season with salt and pepper and serve warm or at room temperature.

Yield: 6 servings

How did the angels get started? I loved the idea of a guardian angel guarding my children. And so I wanted to find something to go over my daughter's bed. I wanted something old and they were horribly expensive, so I thought maybe I'll make one myself. So that's how that began. And I've been shocked at the people…I've heard so many stories. A woman came up to me this weekend and told me she thought my lithograph "An Angel Watches" had saved her child when he had drowned. Her two-year-old had fallen into a swimming pool and they thought he was dead. They did CPR

MEXICAN SALAD BOWL

½ cup celery, sliced
½ cup red onion, coarsely chopped
½ green pepper, coarsely chopped
4 carrots, cut diagonally
6 radishes, sliced
I cup cooled and diced cooked potatoes
I head lettuce
⅓ cup olive oil
¼ cup cider vinegar
½ teaspoon salt
　Black pepper to taste
2 teaspoons granulated sugar
I teaspoon chili powder
¼ teaspoon dried oregano
I medium-sized avocado, sliced
½ cup large stuffed green olives, cut in half
I cup garlic croutons

Mix together celery, onion, green pepper, carrots, radishes and potatoes. Blend together olive oil, vinegar, salt, pepper, sugar, chili powder and oregano. Pour half of dressing over the vegetables. Line salad bowls or plates with lettuce. Heap on vegetables. Top with sliced avocado followed with green olives and croutons. Pour remaining dressing over all.

Yield: 6 servings

and she then looked up and saw my painting and her child woke up.

When I hear stories like that, I believe my angels have a huge impact on people. And I do believe that because of what's happened in my life. There's something out there bigger than I am that's kinda taking care, guarding me and protecting me. I mean, there's no other answer to so many things and then when I hear stories like that, it makes the angels I paint mean so much more. So I'll probably always be painting angels.

BARLEY SALAD WITH ROASTED PEPPERS AND ARUGULA

- 1 cup barley
- 3 tablespoons red wine vinegar
- ½ teaspoon salt
  Pinch of black pepper
- ¼ cup olive oil
- 1 each red and yellow bell peppers, roasted, peeled, seeded, and diced
- 1 cup baby arugula
- ¼ cup pine nuts, toasted
  Salt and black pepper to taste

Place barley in a large pot of lightly salted water. Bring to a boil, lower heat and simmer 15-20 minutes until grains are tender. Combine vinegar, salt, and pepper in bowl and slowly whisk in olive oil. Drain barley and immediately toss with the vinaigrette and bell peppers. Set aside to cool. Just before serving, toss in arugula and pine nuts; season to taste with salt and pepper.

Yield: 6 servings

LENTIL SALAD

2	cups lentils
4	cups water
¾	cup carrots, small dice
½	cup celery, small dice
I	cup red onion, small dice
¼	pound white mushrooms, thinly sliced
2	teaspoons Dijon mustard
2	teaspoons salt, or to taste
¼	cup red wine vinegar
½	cup olive oil

Simmer lentils in water about 25 minutes or until tender. Rinse lentils in cold water until slightly chilled. Drain well. Combine lentils, carrots, celery, onion, and mushrooms. Combine mustard, salt, and vinegar. Stream in olive oil while whisking to fully combine. Toss dressing with lentil mixture.

Cook's Note: *For a colorful salad, serve with tomatoes and avocados.*

Yield: 8 servings

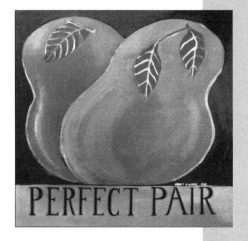

PERFECT PAIR

GRILLED PEAR SALAD WITH PORT VINAIGRETTE

8	ounces sliced, center-cut bacon
3	Bosc pears, sliced into ¼-inch thick slices
	Vegetable oil
	Salt and black pepper
2	cups ruby Port
¼	cup thinly sliced shallot
1	cup extra-virgin olive oil
3	tablespoons red wine vinegar
1½	cups mesclun mix
½	cup crumbled Roquefort cheese
¾	cup pecan halves, toasted

Cook bacon until crisp. Remove from pan and coarsely chop. Heat grill pan or broiler. Coat pear slices with a bit of vegetable oil and sprinkle with salt and pepper. Grill or broil slices about 2 minutes per side until brown in spots. Bring Port and shallot to a boil in heavy medium saucepan. Reduce heat to medium low and simmer about 10 minutes until reduced to ½ cup. Strain into a bowl and cool. Whisk in oil and vinegar and season to taste with salt and pepper. Combine greens, cheese, pecans, bacon and pears in large bowl. Add enough of vinaigrette to lightly coat all ingredients and toss gently. Divide among plates and serve.

Cook's Note: *Unusual and wonderful, this salad is a standout with beef, pork, or chicken!*

Yield: 6 servings

I have a painting in a movie called Mean Street. It's for the kids, the hot movie for teenagers. Anyway, there's a huge painting—I think it's "The March Hare." All My Children has a couple of large prints too. I don't know how it happens.

SPINACH, GRANNY SMITH, AND CHEDDAR CHEESE SALAD

¼ cup balsamic vinegar
¼ cup pure maple syrup
    Salt and black pepper
¼ cup olive oil
2 (6-ounce) packages baby spinach leaves
2 large unpeeled Granny Smith apples,
    halved, cored, thinly sliced
8 ounces extra-sharp Cheddar cheese, cut
    into ½-inch cubes
½ cup chopped toasted walnuts

Combine vinegar, maple syrup, and oil in small bowl; whisk to blend. Season dressing to taste with salt and pepper. Combine spinach, apples, cheese, and walnuts in large bowl. Toss with enough dressing to coat. Season salad to taste with salt and pepper. Transfer salad to serving bowl.

Cook's Note: *A tangy winter salad — try it with a hearty soup and biscuits. The dressing may be made 1 day ahead. Re-whisk to blend before using.*

Yield: 8 servings

It's one of these things that in a million years, I could never have dreamed that my life would have turned out the way it did.

FRESH FRUIT SALAD WITH ORANGE LIQUEUR DRESSING

2	fresh peaches, peeled and sliced
1-2	fresh mangoes, peeled and chopped
1	cup fresh blueberries
1	cup cantaloupe balls
1	cup sliced fresh strawberries
1	cup seedless green grapes
3-4	kiwifruit, peeled and sliced
3	tablespoons orange-flavored liqueur
⅔	cup sour cream
4	tablespoons packed brown sugar, divided

Combine fruit and toss gently with liqueur. Combine sour cream and 3 tablespoons brown sugar. Set dressing aside. Serve fruit mixture with sour cream dressing. Sprinkle with 1 tablespoon brown sugar.

Yield: 6 servings

I started painting watermelons because I love the shape of them, the color of them. And I love the taste of them.

ENDIVE AND WATERCRESS SALAD WITH WALNUTS AND CRANBERRIES

6 cups Belgian endive, trimmed, sliced crosswise into 1-inch pieces
2 bunches watercress, thick stems trimmed
1 tablespoon apple cider vinegar
2 teaspoons Dijon mustard
6 tablespoons olive oil
1 teaspoon mustard seeds
Salt and black pepper, to taste
½ cup walnuts, toasted
½ cup dried cranberries

Place endive and watercress in large bowl. Mix vinegar and mustard in small bowl; slowly whisk in oil. Add mustard seeds. Season dressing with salt and pepper. Pour dressing over endive and watercress; toss to coat. Transfer salad to platter. Sprinkle with walnuts and cranberries and serve.

Yield: 6 servings

CURRIED CHICKEN AND RICE SALAD

½ cup mayonnaise or salad dressing
½ cup plain yogurt
2 teaspoons curry powder
½ teaspoon salt
2 cups cold cooked rice
2 cups cut-up cooked chicken
2 medium mangoes, cut lengthwise in half, pitted and diced (2 cups)
2 medium stalks celery, sliced
1 small bell pepper, chopped

Mix mayonnaise, yogurt, curry powder, and salt in large bowl. Stir in rice, chicken, mangoes, celery, and bell pepper. Cover and refrigerate about 2 hours or until chilled.

Yield: 6 servings

SUMMER RICE SALAD

1	cup rice
4	pear or plum tomatoes, sliced
6	marinated artichoke hearts, thinly sliced
1	(6-ounce) can tuna, drained
3	stalks celery, coarsely chopped
1	small bunch arugula, finely chopped
4	large leaves romaine lettuce (or any other pale green lettuce) cut into small pieces
¼	cup chopped onions
2	anchovies, broken into small pieces (optional)
2	tablespoons capers
⅓	cup black olives, pitted and thinly sliced
3	basil leaves, coarsely chopped
¾	cup olive oil or less
3	tablespoons red wine vinegar
1	tablespoon mayonnaise (optional)
	Salt and black pepper

Cook rice according to directions on package. Set aside to cool for at least 30 minutes. In large bowl, combine tomatoes, artichokes, tuna, celery, arugula, lettuce, onion, anchovies, capers, olives, and basil. Add rice and toss well to combine. In a small jar, shake olive oil and vinegar. Add mayonnaise to dressing if desired. Season with salt and pepper, to taste. Mix well. Pour dressing over salad, a little at a time, tossing well to combine, just until enough dressing coats all ingredients.

Yield: 4 servings

SUMMER

ASPEN SALAD

SALAD
6	chicken breasts, boneless, skinless, cubed, sautéed
2	crisp apples, sliced
2	stalks celery, sliced
8	cups assorted salad greens
½	cup slivered almonds or walnuts, toasted
½	cup currants
4	ounces Gorgonzola cheese, crumbled

DRESSING
¼	cup vegetable oil
¼	cup apple cider
¼	cup white wine vinegar
2	tablespoons maple syrup
1	teaspoon salt
½	teaspoon paprika
1	teaspoon ground mustard
¼	teaspoon freshly ground black pepper

Mix cooked chicken, apples, celery, and salad greens. Make dressing by combining oil with remaining ingredients. Pour dressing over salad mixture and toss lightly. Serve on plates and sprinkle with nuts, currants, and cheese. Spoon over just a little remaining dressing.

Yield: 6 servings

When I was in grade school, my mother and father lost everything in a fire and all my paintings were gone, but I remember a painting I'd done won first place in a show for children at Thalhimer's in Richmond.

CHICKEN PASTA SALAD

SALAD

¼	pound rotelle or other spiral pasta, cooked al dente
1	whole skinless, boneless chicken breast (about ¾ pound), poached and cut into bite-sized pieces (about 1½ cups)
5	cherry tomatoes, quartered
2	scallions, thinly sliced
1	tablespoon finely chopped fresh basil leaves

DRESSING

½	teaspoon minced garlic
1	teaspoon minced peeled fresh gingerroot
1	tablespoon unsalted butter
¼	cup heavy cream
1	tablespoon white wine vinegar
¾	teaspoon curry powder
	Dried, hot red pepper flakes to taste
1	tablespoon finely chopped, drained, bottled mango chutney, or to taste
	Salt and freshly ground black pepper

In a large kettle of boiling salted water, cook pasta for 10 minutes, or until tender. Refresh it in a colander under cold water and drain well. In a large bowl, combine pasta, chicken, tomatoes, scallions, and basil. To make the dressing, cook garlic and gingerroot in butter in a skillet over moderately low heat, stirring, until the garlic is softened. Add cream and cook mixture, whisking, until thickened slightly. Whisk in vinegar, curry powder, red pepper flakes, and chutney. Add dressing to the pasta mixture, tossing the salad to combine it well. Season salad with salt and pepper.

Yield: 2 servings

TURKEY, BLACK BEAN, AND ORZO SALAD

DRESSING
3	tablespoons fresh lime juice
1½	tablespoons white wine vinegar
2	large cloves garlic, minced and mashed to a paste with ½ teaspoon salt
1-2	fresh jalapeño chilies, seeded and chopped (wear rubber gloves), or hot pepper sauce to taste
1½	teaspoons ground cumin, or to taste
	Salt and black pepper
⅔	cup olive oil

SALAD
½	pound (about 1¼ cups) orzo
½	whole poached turkey breast, skin and bone discarded, and meat cut into bite sized pieces (about 4 cups)
1	red bell pepper, finely chopped
1	yellow bell pepper, finely chopped
1	red onion, quartered lengthwise and sliced thin crosswise (about 1½ cups)
1	(15-ounce) can black beans, rinsed well and drained
⅓	cup finely chopped fresh cilantro
	Shredded romaine for lining platter
3	avocados, diced

NOVEMBER

To prepare the dressing, in a blender or small food processor blend together lime juice, vinegar, garlic paste, jalapeños to taste, cumin, salt, and pepper to taste until the mixture is smooth. With the motor running add oil in a stream and blend dressing until emulsified. To cook orzo place in a large saucepan of salted boiling water and cook until al dente. Drain in a colander and rinse under cold water. Let orzo cool and in a large bowl toss it with the turkey, bell peppers, onion, beans, cilantro, and dressing. Arrange romaine on a large platter, spoon turkey salad over it and scatter diced avocados on top.

Cook's Note: *A wonderful summer supper. May also be made with chicken.*

Yield: 6-8 servings

SPICED PORK TENDERLOIN SALAD

PORK
- 2 teaspoons salt
- ½ teaspoon black pepper
- 1 teaspoon ground cumin
- 1 teaspoon chili powder
- 1 teaspoon ground cinnamon
- 2 pork tenderloins (about 2 pounds)
- 2 tablespoons olive oil

GLAZE
- 1 cup packed light brown sugar
- 2 tablespoons minced garlic
- 1 tablespoon hot pepper sauce

VINAIGRETTE
- 3 tablespoons fresh lime juice
- 1 tablespoon fresh orange juice
- 1 tablespoon Dijon mustard
- 1 teaspoon toasted curry powder
- ½ teaspoon salt
- ½ teaspoon black pepper
- ½ cup olive oil

SALAD
- 3 naval oranges
- 5 ounces baby spinach (6 cups leaves)
- 4 cups thinly sliced Napa cabbage
- 1 red bell pepper, cut into thin strips
- 2 firm-ripe avocados

Preheat oven to 350°. Stir together salt, pepper, cumin, chili powder, and cinnamon and coat pork with spice mixture. Heat olive oil in a heavy 12-inch skillet over medium high heat. When oil is hot, add pork, browning well on all sides. Remove pan from heat, keeping tenderloins in skillet. For glaze, stir together brown sugar, garlic, and pepper sauce. Pat this glaze mixture onto top of each tenderloin. Place skillet in oven and cook about 20 minutes. While pork is roasting, whisk together lime juice, orange juice, mustard, curry powder, salt, and pepper. Slowly add oil, whisking constantly, until mixture is well combined. Set aside. To prepare salad ingredients, peel oranges and cut crosswise into ¼-inch thick slices. Toss spinach, cabbage, and pepper in a large bowl with about ¼-cup vinaigrette. Halve, pit, and peel avocados and cut diagonally into ¼-inch thick slices. To assemble salad, cut cooled pork at a 45-degree angle into ½-inch thick slices. Line a large platter with dressed salad and arrange pork, oranges, and avocados in rows on the top. Drizzle oranges and avocados with additional vinaigrette and pour juices from skillet over meat.

Yield: 6-8 servings

GRILLED STEAK SALAD

1	pound slender green beans, trimmed (or haricots verts)
6	cups mesclun or mixed greens
4	cups cherry tomatoes, halved
½	cup olive oil
3-4	tablespoons balsamic vinegar
	Salt and coarse ground black pepper
3	(8- to 9-ounce) New York strip steaks
1	cup crumbled blue cheese
	Freshly ground black pepper

Cook green beans in boiling water until crisp-tender, about 4 minutes. Drain and cool in ice water. Drain and set aside. Combine beans, lettuce, and tomatoes. Whisk oil and vinegar in small bowl. Season with salt and pepper. Grill steaks to desired doneness, about 4 minutes per side for medium rare. Cut steaks crosswise into strips. Toss salad with oil and vinegar. Add tomatoes. Serve on plates, topped with steak strips and crumbled cheese. Drizzle additional oil and vinegar mixture over salad. Sprinkle with freshly ground black pepper and serve.

Cook's Note: *A cool and hearty summer supper.*

Yield: 6 servings

LAURA'S COUSCOUS SHRIMP SALAD

1	(10-ounce) box original plain couscous
1	cup chicken broth or water
1	tablespoon olive oil
1	pound medium shrimp, peeled, deveined, cooked
2	teaspoons seafood seasoning
1	(10-ounce) package frozen peas, thawed completely, rinsed
½	cup peeled, finely diced or shredded carrots
1	tablespoon chopped parsley
2	teaspoons lemon juice
¾	cup mayonnaise
	Salt and black pepper to taste

Cook couscous in chicken broth or water and olive oil according to package directions. Allow to cool. Cook peeled, deveined shrimp in boiling water with seafood seasoning until just pink, about 5 minutes. Drain, and cool completely, cut into bite-size pieces and combine with peas, carrots, parsley, and lemon juice. Combine mayonnaise with shrimp mixture, add couscous, mixing well and season with salt and pepper. Serve chilled.

Yield: 8 servings

CRAB SALAD

1	pound Back Fin crab
1	cup chopped celery
½	cup mayonnaise
1	tablespoon lemon juice
1	tablespoon capers
	Salt and black pepper to taste

Lightly mix all ingredients in a bowl and chill. Serve with your favorite crackers or toasted bread.

Cook's Note: *A perfect crab salad needs scant embellishment, but the addition of capers lends a tangy and very pleasing flavor.*

Yield: 4 servings

My first check was for $7.00. I felt so wonderful.

LOBSTER AND BLACK BEAN SALAD

SALAD
2	(10-ounce) cans black beans
1	pound lobster meat
4	medium stalks celery, diced
1	small red onion, diced
1	medium red bell pepper, diced
1	medium green bell pepper, diced

DRESSING
¼	cup olive oil
3	tablespoons lemon juice
2	tablespoons balsamic vinegar
¼	tablespoon oregano
¼	tablespoon basil
¼	tablespoon cayenne pepper
¼	tablespoon black pepper
1	clove garlic, puréed
2	scallions
6	lettuce leaves

I got serious about painting when my mother died...I think I saw my own mortality and decided I better do it.

Mix beans, lobster, celery, onion, and peppers together in a medium bowl. Mix all dressing ingredients together in a separate bowl. Stir well. Add dressing to lobster mixture. Cover and refrigerate for several hours before serving. Garnish with scallions and serve on lettuce leaves.

Cook's Note: *If desired, shrimp may be used instead of lobster.*

Yield: 4-6 servings

GRILLED TUNA SALADE NIÇOISE

DRESSING
¼ cup red wine vinegar
1½ tablespoons minced shallot
2 teaspoons Dijon mustard
1 large clove garlic, minced
½ teaspoon (rounded) anchovy paste
1 cup extra-virgin olive oil
1½ teaspoons minced fresh thyme
1½ tablespoons finely chopped fresh basil
   Salt and black pepper to taste

SALAD
¾ pound green beans, trimmed
1½ pounds small (1- to 2-inch) potatoes
6 ¼ pound each (1-inch thick) tuna steaks
   Peanut oil for brushing
¼ cup drained bottled capers
2 heads Boston lettuce, leaves separated and large ones torn into pieces
3 tablespoons finely chopped fresh parsley and/or basil
1 pint cherry or grape tomatoes
⅔ cup niçoise or other small brine-cured black olives
6 hard-boiled eggs, quartered

For dressing, whisk together vinegar, shallot, mustard, garlic, and anchovy paste in small bowl until combined well. Add oil in slow stream, whisking until emulsified. Whisk in thyme, basil, salt, and pepper. For salad, cook beans in 4- to 6-quart pot of boiling water, uncovered, until crisp-tender (3-4 minutes), immediately transfer with slotted spoon to a bowl of ice cold water to stop cooking. Add potatoes to boiling water and simmer, uncovered, until tender (15-20 minutes). Drain in colander. Halve potatoes while still warm and toss with 2 tablespoons of dressing in a bowl. Allow to cool. Brush tuna with oil and season with salt and pepper. Pan fry in pan lightly oiled with cooking spray over medium-high heat for 3-4 minutes per side. (Or grill over medium-high heat for

I've traveled a lot and it's so interesting to see these farm co-ops. Grocery stores are starting to get together and they'll have farmers who grow food just for them. And you get fresher, more organic food and, as you all know, there's a huge difference in food that's grown like that and food that's shipped around the country. I haven't eaten a tomato in ages that tastes the way I remember them. Now they're just hybrids.

6-8 minutes total.) Transfer tuna to a platter and drizzle with 2-3 tablespoons of dressing and top with capers. Transfer potatoes to platter with tuna, reserving bowl. Drain beans and pat dry. Toss beans in bowl with 1 tablespoon dressing, salt, and pepper to taste, then transfer to platter. Toss lettuce in same manner with 2 tablespoons dressing, salt, pepper and transfer to platter. Toss tomatoes as above with 1 tablespoon dressing, salt, pepper and transfer to platter. Arrange olives and eggs on platter and sprinkle with parsley and/or basil and remaining dressing.

Cook's Note: *This is a beautiful salad to serve for guests.*

Yield: 6 servings

RED WINE MUSTARD VINAIGRETTE

¼	cup water
6	tablespoons red wine vinegar
½	teaspoon granulated sugar
2½	teaspoons lemon juice
1¼	teaspoons salt, or to taste
½	teaspoon freshly ground black pepper, or to taste
½	teaspoon coarse grain mustard
2	cloves garlic, minced
1¼	cups extra-virgin olive oil

Combine together all of the ingredients except for the olive oil. Allow the flavors to blend for 5 minutes. Add the olive oil, whisking thoroughly. It may be necessary to blend the dressing together again before serving.

Cook's Note: *May be used for most green salads.*

Yield: 2 cups

I'm afraid to be too secure because... I'm not secure. It has nothing to do with selling. I don't consider myself a master at it...I'm always learning. There's always a way to stretch and challenge yourself. You have to do that. That's why I think it's very important to take those risks.

LEMON-PARSLEY VINAIGRETTE

- ¾ cup lemon juice
- 2 tablespoons balsamic vinegar
- ¾ cup canola oil
- 5½ tablespoons olive oil
- 1½ tablespoons parsley, chopped
- 1 teaspoon salt, or to taste
- ½ teaspoon freshly ground black pepper, or to taste

Combine all of the ingredients in a large bowl and, using a whisk, mix all ingredients until thoroughly incorporated.

Cook's Note: *A versatile dressing for most green salads.*

Yield: 2 cups

POPPY SEED DRESSING

- ¾ cup granulated sugar
- ⅓ cup cider vinegar
- 1 cup canola oil
- 1 tablespoon Dijon mustard
- 1 tablespoon poppy seeds

Combine all of the ingredients in a medium bowl and, using a whisk, mix all ingredients until thoroughly incorporated.

Cook's Note: *Serve over spinach and strawberry salad or on grapefruit, orange or fresh pear salad.*

Yield: 2 cups

Accompaniments

ACCOMPANIMENTS

ASPARAGUS GRATIN WITH PARMESAN CHEESE

3	quarts salted water
24	medium-size asparagus spears
½	cup freshly grated Parmesan cheese
2	tablespoons fine plain dry breadcrumbs
½	teaspoon grated lemon zest
3	tablespoons unsalted butter, melted

Bring the salted water to a boil in a large saucepan. Trim the woody ends from the asparagus spears. With a vegetable peeler, peel the bottom half of the spears. Add the asparagus to the boiling water and cook until tender but still crisp, about 6 minutes. Drain well. In a small bowl, toss the cheese, breadcrumbs, and lemon zest together until blended. Preheat the broiler. Arrange the asparagus stalks in a single layer in an 8-inch square or similar-size flameproof baking dish. Drizzle the asparagus with the melted butter and sprinkle an even layer of the breadcrumb mixture over it. Broil about 4 inches from the heat for about 3 minutes until the breadcrumb mixture is golden brown. Serve hot.

Cook's Note: *Can be completely assembled in a baking dish and then broiled just before serving.*

Yield: 6 servings

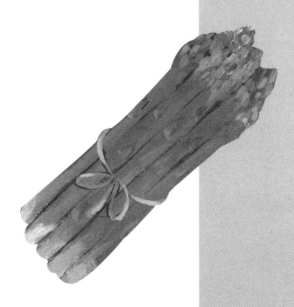

I feel less secure now as an artist than I've ever felt. I'm trying to do things differently than I've done in the past. I'm experimenting. And I'm trying to go places I've never been before. I'm not afraid, even if I'm just painting to learn. I'll paint something and if it doesn't work out, I have zero problem painting over something.

SESAME BALSAMIC ASPARAGUS

2   pounds asparagus spears
1½   teaspoons dark sesame oil
2   teaspoons soy sauce
1   teaspoon balsamic vinegar
¼   teaspoon kosher or sea salt
⅛   teaspoon freshly ground black pepper
      Grated Parmesan cheese
      Sesame seeds

Preheat oven to 450°. Snap off tough ends of the asparagus spears and place spears in one layer on a jelly-roll pan. Whisk together sesame seed oil, soy sauce, and balsamic vinegar. Drizzle mixture over asparagus, turning asparagus to coat. Sprinkle with salt and pepper. Bake at 450° for 10-12 minutes or until the asparagus are crisp tender. Sprinkle with fresh Parmesan cheese and sesame seeds and serve immediately.

Cook's Note: *When roasting asparagus, the fatter the spears, the better they roast.*

Yield: 4-6 servings

GREEN BEANS VINAIGRETTE

3   pounds fresh green beans
½   cup olive oil
3   tablespoons red wine vinegar
1   teaspoon Dijon mustard
½   teaspoon salt
¼   teaspoon freshly ground black pepper
1   large red onion, thinly sliced

Steam green beans in a large pot for 7-8 minutes or to taste. Drain and pat dry. In a large bowl, mix oil, vinegar, mustard, salt, and pepper into a vinaigrette. Add red onion slices. Add beans and toss to coat. Serve immediately or refrigerate and serve cold.

Yield: 10-12 servings

ASPARAGUS
WITH GARLIC MUSTARD

I	pound asparagus spears, trimmed
1/4	cup butter or margarine
2	cups sliced fresh button mushrooms
2	tablespoons Dijon mustard
1/4	teaspoon freshly ground black pepper
1/8	teaspoon salt
I	teaspoon minced garlic

In a 10-inch skillet, place asparagus spears. Add enough water to cover. Bring to a full boil. Cook over medium heat 7 minutes or until asparagus is tender crisp. Drain. Remove from skillet. Add butter, mushrooms, mustard, pepper, salt, and garlic pushing asparagus to the side just until butter is melted. Cook over medium heat, stirring occasionally, until thoroughly heated.

Yield: 4 servings

GREEN BEANS
WITH FETA CHEESE

I	pound green beans
1/2	cup olive oil
1/4	cup white wine vinegar
1/2	cup fresh mint leaves
	Salt and black pepper
1/2	cup chopped walnuts, toasted
I	small red onion, chopped
I	cup crumbled feta cheese

Cook beans in boiling water about 8 minutes or until crisp tender. Rinse under cold water and drain. Mix oil, vinegar, mint leaves, salt, and pepper to taste in blender. When ready to serve, toss beans with oil mixture and walnuts, onion, and cheese.

Yield: 6 servings

HONEY GLAZED GREEN BEANS AMANDINE

4	cups fresh green beans
1	tablespoon butter or margarine
1	tablespoon honey
1/4	teaspoon ground nutmeg
	Salt and black pepper, to taste
1/2	cup toasted almond slivers

Prepare green beans by slicing the ends at an angle. Boil or steam for about 8 minutes, or until tender. Drain and place on serving dish. Melt butter over low heat and add honey, nutmeg, salt, and pepper. Stir into green beans. Garnish with toasted almond slivers.

Yield: 6 servings

SANTA FE BLACK BEANS

3	tablespoons olive oil
1	medium onion, chopped
4-6	cloves garlic, minced
1	(15-ounce) can black beans, drained
1	(15-ounce) can Italian tomatoes, chopped
1	cup fresh grape tomatoes
2-4	tablespoons ground cumin
1	teaspoon cumin seeds, ground in a spice grinder
1/4	cup fresh cilantro or fresh oregano, chopped
1/4	cup shredded Cheddar cheese

In a medium saucepan, heat olive oil over medium heat. Add onions stirring occasionally until translucent and golden. Add garlic and stir until fragrant. Add black beans, tomatoes, cumin and cumin seeds. Cover and simmer for 30-40 minutes over low heat. Add cilantro or oregano, and cheese. Serve hot.

Cook's Note: *This may also be pulsed to a chunky purée in the food processor and served as a hot dip, topped with the cheese and served with tortilla chips.*

Yield: 4 servings

BEETS WITH LIME BUTTER

3	tablespoons unsalted butter, divided
1½	pounds beets, peeled and coarsely grated (3½ cups)
¼	teaspoon finely grated lime zest
1	tablespoon fresh lime juice, or to taste
¾	teaspoon salt
¼	teaspoon freshly ground black pepper
	Finely chopped scallion greens for garnish

Melt 2 tablespoons butter in a 10-inch heavy skillet over moderately high heat. Add beets and lime zest and cook, stirring about 5 minutes or until beets are crisp tender. Remove skillet from heat and stir in remaining 1 tablespoon of butter, lime juice, salt, and pepper. Serve garnished with scallion greens, if desired.

Yield: 4 servings

BAKED PARMESAN BRUSSELS SPROUTS

1½	pounds Brussels sprouts
2	tablespoons olive oil
4	tablespoons butter
2	cloves garlic, minced
	Kosher salt
	Freshly ground black pepper
	Parmesan cheese, shaved

Preheat oven to 350°. Cut sprouts in half lengthwise and peel tough outer leaves. Melt the oil and butter in a saucepan and stir in garlic. Add the sprouts and season with salt and pepper. Pour into a baking sheet in an even layer and bake approximately 30 minutes or until soft. Shave Parmesan using a vegetable peeler. Cover sprouts lightly with shaved Parmesan slices during the last few minutes of cooking.

Yield: 6 servings

112

SWISS CHARD GRATIN

2	teaspoons softened butter plus 2 tablespoons butter
⅓	cup fresh breadcrumbs, divided
I	tablespoon olive oil
¼	cup finely chopped shallot
I	tablespoon minced garlic
I	pound Swiss chard, stems sliced in ½-inch pieces, washed but not dried
	Salt and black pepper
2	tablespoons all-purpose flour
I½	cups milk
I	dried bay leaf
	Pinch of freshly grated nutmeg
2	tablespoons finely chopped fresh oregano or 2 teaspoons dried oregano
2	teaspoons finely chopped fresh thyme or ¾ teaspoon dried thyme
I	cup grated Gruyère cheese, divided
	Salt and freshly ground black pepper

There are certain things I'm insecure about. The problem is, I'm not sure what I want. I'm torn right now, and I've got to get over this, really fast, of wanting to make things look more realistic… but I don't. And Sydney's a wonderful help to me. He's a true artist, he really is, and he does crazy things, but he's a true artist. He said he's had that struggle too and he was trying to paint things that looked more real. He said it was torture for him, and it's torture

Coat the inside of a I½-quart baking dish with the 2 teaspoons of softened butter. Sprinkle with 2 tablespoons of the breadcrumbs, coating the dish evenly. Preheat the oven to 400°. Heat the olive oil in a large pot over medium heat. Add the shallot and garlic and cook, stirring constantly for about I minute or until softened and lightly browned. Add the damp chard to the pot, and cover tightly. Cook for 2 or 3 minutes or until the chard is about half of its original volume. Remove the lid and turn the chard with a pair of tongs. Continue cooking until all of the water in the pan has evaporated. Sprinkle with salt and pepper and set aside. Melt the remaining 2 tablespoons of butter in a small saucepan over medium heat. Whisk in the flour and continue whisking for about I minute or until the mixture bubbles up and turns pale in color. Pour in the milk all at once while whisking vigorously. Add a pinch of salt, bay leaf, and nutmeg and continue to whisk the sauce until it boils and thickens. Reduce the heat to low and simmer the sauce for about 2 minutes. Stir in the oregano, thyme and ½ cup of the grated Gruyère. Remove and discard the bay leaf. Stir the sauce into the chard mixture.

Taste and add additional salt or pepper if necessary. Spoon the mixture into the prepared dish. Sprinkle the top with the remaining breadcrumbs and cheese. Bake about 25-35 minutes in preheated oven until the mixture bubbles and the top is nicely browned.

Yield: 4-6 servings

PAN-BROWNED BRUSSELS SPROUTS

1½	tablespoons unsalted butter, divided
1	tablespoon olive oil
2	large cloves garlic, thinly sliced
½	pound Brussels sprouts, trimmed and halved lengthwise
2	tablespoons pine nuts
	Salt and freshly ground black pepper

Melt 1 tablespoon of butter with oil in a 10-inch heavy skillet over moderate heat. Add garlic and cook, stirring until pale gold in color, about 3 minutes. With a slotted spoon, transfer to a small bowl. Reduce heat to low, arrange sprouts cut sides down in skillet in one layer, and sprinkle with pine nuts and salt and pepper to taste. Cook, uncovered, without turning, until sprouts are crisp tender and undersides are golden brown about 10-15 minutes. With tongs, transfer sprouts, browned sides up, to a plate, leaving pine nuts in pan. Add remaining ½ tablespoon butter to skillet and cook nuts over moderate heat, stirring until evenly pale golden, or about 1 minute. Stir in garlic and spoon mixture over sprouts.

Yield: 2 servings

for me. And he just decided that's not what he's supposed to be doing. He's happy as a lark now, he does what he wants to do and he's prolific. That helped me tremendously because I thought, why am I trying to put myself into this little mold when I really should be allowing myself to be freer and do what I want to do…I don't really know what that is, but I just do it!

CARAWAY CABBAGE

2	tablespoons butter
1	small head of cabbage, coarsely shredded
1	teaspoon salt
1	clove garlic, minced
1	teaspoon caraway seeds
1	teaspoon granulated sugar or Splenda
1½	tablespoons cider vinegar
½	cup sour cream

Melt butter in a skillet. Add the cabbage, salt and garlic, stirring well. Cover tightly with a fitted lid and steam for 10 minutes. It may be necessary to add about ⅛ cup of water. Remove cover and add caraway seeds, sugar, and vinegar mixing well. Stir in the sour cream, heat and serve.

Cook's Note: *Delicious for a low carb dinner.*

Yield: 4 servings

GINGERED CARROTS

2	pounds baby carrots
6	tablespoons ginger marmalade or preserves
6	tablespoons butter
6	tablespoons fresh lemon juice
1	teaspoon salt
½	teaspoon black pepper

Boil carrots for 8-10 minutes, drain. Combine the marmalade, butter, lemon juice, and salt in a small saucepan. Cook over medium heat for 2-3 minutes or until syrupy. Add the carrots, coat with sauce and cook for 5-7 minutes. Season with pepper.

Cook's Note: *Using the marmalade gives a wonderful ginger flavor. One tablespoon of ground ginger may be substituted, but the flavor will be less gingery.*

Yield: 6-8 servings

GLAZED LEMON CARROTS

2	cups baby carrots
4	tablespoons butter
I	teaspoon granulated sugar
½	teaspoon light brown sugar
½	teaspoon paprika
I	tablespoon lemon juice
I	teaspoon minced fresh parsley for garnish

Cook carrots in boiling water until just fork tender. Drain carrots and set aside. Melt butter in sauté pan, add both sugars, paprika, and lemon juice. Mix well. Stir in carrots; shake pan to completely glaze carrots. Garnish with parsley.

Yield: 4-6 servings

PINK PICKLED ONIONS

2	pounds red onions, thinly sliced, separated into rings, divided
6	(4-inch) fresh rosemary sprigs
2	cups champagne vinegar or white wine vinegar
I½	cups water
I	cup granulated sugar
I	heaping tablespoon mixed pickling spice
2	teaspoons Kosher salt

Place ⅓ of the onions in large jar with tight-fitting lid. Add I rosemary sprig. Repeat layering twice more with remaining onions and rosemary. Bring vinegar, I½ cups water, sugar, pickling spice, and salt to boil in a medium saucepan over high heat, stirring until sugar dissolves. Reduce heat and simmer 2 minutes, stirring often. Pour hot liquid over onions, pushing onions down into liquid. If necessary, add just enough cold water to cover onions. Cool. Place lid on jar; refrigerate at least I day. Can be made 2 weeks ahead. Keep chilled.

Cook's Note: *For a unique cook-out, serve these with assorted grilled gourmet sausages, spicy mustard and pita bread instead of rolls. Keep in the refrigerator for up to 2 weeks.*

Yield: 8 cups

ROASTED CORN
WITH GRAPE TOMATOES

3	ears of corn, shucked and cleaned of silks
	Olive oil for brushing corn
	Pinch of Kosher salt
2	pints grape tomatoes
¼	cup extra virgin olive oil
½	teaspoon dried thyme
½	teaspoon dried oregano
1¼	teaspoons kosher salt
3	ounces Ricotta-Salata cheese or feta cheese

I feel I should have more confidence in myself as an artist, and I try to come across as if I have confidence, but underneath it all, and that's where it all is, there's the insecurity.

Preheat the oven to 400°. Brush cleaned ears of corn with olive oil and season with salt. Roast the corn directly over a flame until it begins to turn golden. Rotate every 30 seconds. Transfer to a cooling rack to cool. Cut the corn away from the cob. If the corn seems dry, drizzle with a little olive oil and toss to coat. Set the corn aside. Wash the tomatoes and toss in olive oil, dried thyme, dried oregano and salt. Roast the tomatoes for about 10-12 minutes or until they release their juices and soften. Remove from the oven and cool slightly. Add the cooled corn and cheese.

Cook's Note: *Corn may be roasted in a 500° oven for 15 minutes, turning once.*

Yield: 8 servings

0# HERBED GLAZED ONIONS

- 2 pounds small white onions in their skin
- 6 tablespoons butter
- ½ cup light brown sugar
- 2 tablespoons water for the glaze
- 1 teaspoon salt
- ½ teaspoon black pepper
- 2 tablespoons fresh thyme or rosemary, chopped

Boil onions in water for 10-11 minutes. Drain and plunge into cold water. Trim root ends and slip off skin. In a large heavy skillet, heat the butter, brown sugar, water, salt, pepper, and thyme or rosemary. Cook 3-4 minutes or until syrupy. Add onions and cook for 5-6 minutes or until glazed.

Yield: 6 servings

OLD FASHIONED CREAMED ONIONS

Bon Appetit

- 2 tablespoons butter
- 2 tablespoons all-purpose flour
- 1 (14-ounce) jar onions, drained with liquid reserved
- 4 ounces extra sharp Cheddar cheese, grated
  Seasoned breadcrumbs

Preheat oven to 350°. Over moderate heat, melt butter and whisk in the flour. Cook for one minute. Slowly add the onion liquid, whisking to make a smooth sauce. Stir in cheese and heat until melted. Add onions, turning to coat. Pour into a 1-quart casserole dish, top with seasoned breadcrumbs and bake for 20-30 minutes until hot and bubbly.

Yield: 4 servings

FARMER'S POTATOES

8   large potatoes
4-8 tablespoons butter, do not substitute
    Seasoning salt to taste
2   (8-ounce) cartons heavy cream

Boil potatoes in their skins until almost done; do not overcook. Peel and allow potatoes to cool. When potatoes are cool, grate or shred finely. Preheat oven to 350°. Place ⅓ of potatoes in the bottom of an ungreased 9x13-inch glass baking dish; top with 6-8 thin pats of butter and a generous sprinkling of seasoned salt. Repeat with 2 more layers. Pour cream over potatoes and bake uncovered 1 hour

Cook's Note: *The cooled potatoes grate very easily. The whipping cream will not cover the potatoes; it bubbles up during cooking. This dish can be prepared early in the day and kept chilled until ready to bake.*

Yield: 12 servings

BRIE-STUFFED JACKET POTATOES

2   Idaho potatoes, baked
3   ounces Brie cheese, rind removed and at
    room temperature
½   teaspoon salt
1   egg yolk
2   ounces butter, room temperature
    Freshly chopped chives

Preheat oven to 375°. Slice potatoes in half and scoop out the flesh into a medium mixing bowl. Place potato jackets on a baking sheet. Mix together potato flesh, Brie, salt, egg yolk and butter. Mix well and return mixture to empty potato jackets. Place into oven and cook for about 15 minutes, until the filling is golden brown. Remove and sprinkle with chopped chives, serving immediately.

Yield: 2 servings

Romantic foods? Mashed potatoes. Actually, that's my comfort food. It relaxes me.

DEVILISH POTATOES

2¾ pounds small red potatoes
(about 1½ inches in diameter)
3 tablespoons vegetable oil
2 teaspoons Kosher salt, divided
¼ cup unsalted butter
2 teaspoons cider vinegar
1 teaspoon Dijon mustard
¼ rounded teaspoon cayenne pepper, or to
taste

Put oven racks in upper and lower thirds of oven and preheat oven to 475°. Put 2 large shallow baking pans (1-inch deep) in oven and preheat 10 minutes. Quarter potatoes, then toss with oil and 1½ teaspoons salt in a large bowl. Spread potatoes, cut sides down, in hot pans, roasting about 12 minutes or until undersides are golden. Turn potatoes so other cut sides are down, then switch position of pans and roast 12-15 minutes more or until potatoes are tender and undersides are golden. While potatoes roast, melt butter in a small saucepan and whisk in vinegar, mustard, cayenne, and remaining ½ teaspoon kosher salt. Toss hot potatoes with butter mixture until coated.

Yield: 10 servings

GARLIC FRIES

1½ pounds peeled baking potatoes, cut into
    ¼-inch thick strips
2 teaspoons vegetable oil
¼ teaspoon salt
  Cooking spray
1 tablespoon butter
4 cloves garlic, minced
1 tablespoon finely chopped fresh parsley
1 tablespoon freshly grated Parmesan cheese

Preheat the oven to 400°. Combine potatoes, oil, and salt in a large zip-top plastic bag, tossing to coat. Arrange potatoes in a single layer on a baking sheet coated with cooking spray. Bake for 40 minutes or until potatoes are tender and golden brown, turning after 20 minutes. Place butter and garlic in a large non-stick skillet; cook over low heat 2 minutes, stirring constantly. Add potatoes, parsley, and cheese to pan; toss to coat. Serve immediately.

Cook's Note: *Tossing the fries in butter and garlic after cooking makes them unbelievably rich.*

Yield: 3 servings

There was an event called "Taste of Virginia" and I was commissioned to do a sculpture as a gift for Governor Wilder to give to the president of Bloomingdale's.

SWEET POTATOES WITH GINGER-MOLASSES BUTTER

- ½ cup unsalted butter, room temperature
- 3 tablespoons golden brown sugar, packed
- I tablespoon mild-flavored light molasses
- ½ teaspoon ground ginger
- ¼ teaspoon ground cinnamon
  Pinch of ground cloves
- 3 tablespoons minced crystallized ginger
  Salt and black pepper
- 6 (8-ounce) red-skinned sweet potatoes,
  rinsed and patted dry

Preheat oven to 350°. Mix butter, brown sugar, molasses, ginger, cinnamon, and cloves in a small bowl to blend. Stir in crystallized ginger. Season with salt and a generous amount of pepper. Pierce potatoes in several places with a fork; bake on rimmed baking sheet for about 50 minutes or until tender when pierced with a fork. Cut lengthwise slit in each potato and press in ends to open top. Spoon 2 tablespoons ginger-molasses butter onto each potato.

Cook's Note: *Ginger-Molasses Butter may be made 3 days ahead. Refrigerate. Bring to room temperature to use.*

Yield: 6 servings

GRILLED SWEET POTATOES WITH CHIPOTLE HONEY SAUCE

Vegetable cooking spray
6   medium sweet potatoes
⅓   cup olive or vegetable oil
2   teaspoons coarse salt, divided

CHIPOTLE HONEY SAUCE
1   cup honey
4   chipotle chilies in adobo sauce, finely
      chopped
2   tablespoons adobo sauce from can of
      chilies

Spray grill rack with cooking spray. Heat coals on gas grill for direct heat. Cut each sweet potato lengthwise into 4 slices. Brush both sides with oil. Place potatoes on grill rack and sprinkle with 1 teaspoon of the salt. Cover and grill 4-6 inches from medium heat for 8-10 minutes, turning once and sprinkling with remaining salt, until potatoes are tender. While potatoes are cooking, make the Chipotle Honey Sauce by mixing all ingredients together. Top potatoes with sauce and serve.

Yield: 6 servings

GINGER-LIME SWEET POTATOES

⅓   cup all-purpose flour
10   cups thinly sliced peeled sweet potato
        (about 3 pounds)
¼   cup butter
⅓   cup packed light brown sugar
1   tablespoon lime zest
2   tablespoons fresh lime juice
1   tablespoon orange zest
1   tablespoon grated peeled fresh ginger
1   teaspoon low-sodium soy sauce
½   teaspoon salt
¼   teaspoon black pepper
        Cooking spray

Preheat oven to 425°. Lightly spoon flour into a dry measuring cup; level with a knife. Combine flour and potatoes in a large bowl, toss well. Melt butter in a small saucepan over low heat. Add sugar, lime zest, lime juice, orange zest, ginger, soy sauce, salt and pepper. Cook 4 minutes or until sugar dissolves. Pour over potato mixture and toss well. Spoon mixture into a shallow 2-quart casserole dish coated with cooking spray. Cover and bake for 55 minutes or until tender. Let stand 10 minutes.

Cook's Note: *What a pleasant change from the usual sweet potato recipe! The ginger lime gives a new flavor that compliments poultry, pork or even seafood.*

Yield: 12 servings

SPINACH GRATIN

4	tablespoons unsalted butter
4	cups chopped yellow onions
¼	cup all-purpose flour
¼	teaspoon grated nutmeg
3	cups light cream
5	(10-ounce) packages frozen chopped spinach, defrosted
1	cup freshly grated Parmesan cheese, divided
1	tablespoon Kosher salt
½	teaspoon freshly ground black pepper
½	cup grated Gruyère cheese

Preheat the oven to 425°. Melt the butter in a heavy-bottomed sauté pan over medium heat. Add the onions and sauté about 15 minutes or until translucent. Add the flour and nutmeg and cook, stirring for 2 more minutes. Add the cream and cook until thickened. Squeeze as much liquid as possible from the spinach and add the spinach to the sauce. Add ½ cup of the Parmesan cheese and mix well. Season to taste with the salt and pepper. Transfer the spinach to a 2½-quart baking dish and sprinkle the remaining ½ cup Parmesan and the Gruyère on top. Bake for 20 minutes, or until hot and bubbly. Serve immediately.

Cook's Note: *This can be made up to 2 days in advance and refrigerated until ready to bake.*

Yield: 8 servings

PROVENÇAL ROAST TOMATOES

¼ cup extra virgin olive oil

12 firm tomatoes, cored and halved
    lengthwise

    Sea salt to taste

¼ cup fresh mixed herbs, such as parsley
    leaves, tarragon, basil, and rosemary,
    snipped with scissors

¼ cup red wine vinegar

Preheat the oven to 400°. In a very large skillet, heat the oil over moderately high heat. When hot, place as many tomatoes as will easily fit in the pan, cut side down. Do not crowd the pan as the tomatoes will steam, not sear. Sear without moving the tomatoes for 3-4 minutes or until they are dark and almost caramelized. Transfer the tomatoes, cooked side up to a 10x16-inch baking dish. Overlap them slightly since they will reduce as they bake. Continue until all the tomatoes are seared. Season the tomatoes lightly with salt. Remove the pan from the heat and deglaze the remaining fat in the pan with the vinegar. Return the pan to high heat, scraping the bottom of the pan to loosen drippings into the liquid. Pour over the tomatoes. Sprinkle with fresh herbs. Place the baking dish in the center of the oven and bake, uncovered, about 30 minutes or until the tomatoes are soft, shriveled, and even a bit black around the edges. They may be served hot, warm, or even at room temperature.

Yield: 8 servings

The more you paint from truth, the more you will touch people.

126

BAKED HERBED TOMATOES

4-6 small tomatoes
½ cup butter or margarine
½ cup onion, chopped
I clove garlic, minced
¾ cup fine dry breadcrumbs
¼ cup fresh basil, chopped
I tablespoon fresh thyme, chopped
Salt and black pepper

Preheat oven to 350°. Wash tomatoes. Cut a slice from the stem end and cut a cone-shaped piece from the top. Make a vertical slice halfway down each tomato. Gently squeeze out the juice and shake out seeds, being very careful not to break shells. Melt butter in a medium hot skillet. Add onion and garlic and cook until soft. Remove the pan from heat and stir in breadcrumbs, basil, and thyme. Spoon bread mixture onto the tomatoes. Place tomatoes in a shallow baking dish and sprinkle with salt and pepper to taste. Bake for 30 minutes or until the tomatoes are tender.

Yield: 4-6 servings

VIRGINIA FRIED GREEN TOMATOES

Green or pink tomatoes (one per person)
I cup all-purpose flour
⅓ cup granulated sugar
½ teaspoon salt
Bacon fat or shortening

Wash tomatoes, but do not peel them. Slice in ¾-inch slices and thoroughly coat each slice with the flour, sugar, and salt mixture. Melt enough bacon fat (or combination of fats) in a heavy skillet to cover the bottom with ⅛-inch of fat. Add floured tomatoes. Cook slowly over low heat until lightly browned on the bottom. Turn and cook slowly on the other side, adding more fat if necessary. Cooking time is approximately 20 minutes. Serve hot.

Yield: One tomato per person

VERA CRUZ TOMATOES

3 strips bacon
¼ cup chopped onion
8 ounces fresh spinach, washed and drained
1 cup sour cream
4 large tomatoes
   Shredded Cheddar cheese
   Salt and black pepper, to taste

Preheat oven to 375°. Cook bacon until crisp. Drain, reserving 2 tablespoons of bacon grease. Crumble bacon and set aside. Cook onion in reserved drippings until tender. Stir in the spinach. Cook covered for about 5 minutes or until tender. Remove from heat and stir in sour cream and bacon. Cut tops from tomatoes. Remove the centers, leaving shells. Drain. Fill shells with spinach mixture. Place in a baking dish. Bake for 25 minutes. Top with shredded cheese, sprinkle with salt and pepper and return to oven for 2 minutes to melt the cheese.

Yield: 4 servings

ROASTED BALSAMIC ZUCCHINI

4	pounds medium zucchini, cut diagonally into ½-inch slices
¼	cup extra virgin olive oil
¾	teaspoon salt
½	teaspoon coarsely ground black pepper
¼	cup balsamic vinegar
1½	ounces finely grated Parmigiano-Reggiano cheese, divided
⅓	cup pine nuts, toasted and finely chopped

It's not totally conscious, it's more acting on emotions, than thinking it through...and if I'm not doing that, I'm eating.

Preheat the broiler. Toss zucchini with oil, salt, and pepper in a large bowl. Arrange zucchini in 1 layer in 2 shallow baking pans (1-inch deep). Broil 1 pan of zucchini 3-5 inches from heat, without turning, for 4-6 minutes or until browned in spots and beginning to soften. Drizzle 2 tablespoons vinegar over broiled zucchini and shake pan a few times. Continue to broil for about 2 minutes or until most of the vinegar is evaporated. Sprinkle ¼-cup cheese over broiled zucchini and broil approximately 1 minute more or until cheese is melted. Cook remaining pan of zucchini in the same manner. Cool to room temperature and serve sprinkled with pine nuts.

Yield: 6 servings

ZUCCHINI CREOLE

3	slices bacon
2-3	tablespoons chopped onion
1	small green bell pepper, chopped
2	cups sliced zucchini
1	teaspoon granulated sugar
½	teaspoon salt
¼	teaspoon cracked black pepper
½	teaspoon Worcestershire sauce
1	cup tomato, peeled and chopped or 1 cup drained tomato wedges
4	ounces tomato sauce

Fry bacon until crisp. Drain and crumble. Set bacon aside, reserving 1 tablespoon of grease. Sauté onion and green pepper in bacon grease until golden brown. Add zucchini and cook over low heat 3-5 minutes. Add sugar, salt, pepper, Worcestershire, tomatoes and tomato sauce. Cover and cook on medium heat for 10 minutes. Top with bacon to serve.

Cook's Note: *This may be served over rice for a hearty, vegetarian dish.*

Yield: 4 servings

LEMON BROCCOLI RISOTTO

- 4 cups chicken broth, divided
- 2 cups water
- I pound broccoli, cut into flowerets, and quartered if large
- I teaspoon freshly grated lemon zest
- I tablespoon fresh lemon juice
- I small onion, finely chopped
- I small clove garlic, minced
- 2 tablespoons olive oil
- I ½ cups rice, (short, medium, or long-grain)
- ½ cup freshly grated Parmesan cheese
  Salt and white pepper to taste

In a large saucepan bring the broth and the water to a boil and in the broth simmer the broccoli flowerets for 3 minutes or until tender. Drain and reserve flowerets. To the simmering broth add the broccoli stems, the zest, and the lemon juice and simmer the mixture for 5 minutes. While the stems are cooking, in a large heavy saucepan cook the onion and the garlic in oil over moderately low heat, stirring, until the onion is softened. Stir in the rice, stirring until all grains are coated with the oil. Add ½ cup of the simmering broth, stems included, and cook the mixture over moderately high heat, stirring constantly, until the broth is absorbed. Continue adding the broth mixture ½ cup at a time, stirring constantly and letting each portion be absorbed before adding the next, until the rice is tender but still al dente. This should take about 30 minutes. Stir in the reserved broccoli flowerets and simmer the risotto, stirring until the flowerets are heated through. Remove the pan from the heat and stir in the Parmesan and salt and pepper to taste.

Yield: 2 servings

JASMINE RICE PILAF

1	cup wild rice
1	(14-ounce) can chicken broth
1	cup jasmine rice
¼	cup butter
1	cup chopped scallions, green tops included
½	cup diced dried apricots
½	cup coarsely chopped roasted, salted cashews
2	teaspoons lemon zest
	Salt and black pepper, to taste

Cook wild rice in large pot of boiling salted water for about 55 minutes or until just tender. Drain well. Bring broth to a boil in medium saucepan over high heat. Mix in jasmine rice. Reduce heat to medium-low. Cover and cook for about 18 minutes until rice is tender and broth is absorbed. Melt butter in heavy large skillet over medium-high heat. Add onions, apricots, cashews, and lemon peel. Stir about 1 minute or until onions are soft. Add all rice. Toss to blend and heat through for about 3 minutes. Season with salt and pepper.

Yield: 6 servings

Sometimes when I'm painting for the business, it's very tedious and I'm exhausted. If I go in there and start fixing something to eat, a simple meal of any sort, all of it just melts away. Suddenly, I'm in a whole different realm and it's relaxing. Before, the art used to do that for me, and it still does; it's a way of letting go and being creative.

GINGER BASMATI PILAF

2	cups low-sodium chicken stock
1	tablespoon butter
1	cup white basmati rice, rinsed well
2	teaspoons vegetable oil
¼	cup diced carrots
¼	cup thinly sliced scallions
2	cloves garlic, minced
1	tablespoon minced, fresh ginger
2	tablespoons soy sauce
1	teaspoon ground coriander

In a medium saucepan, boil chicken stock. Stir in butter and rice. Cover, reduce heat to low, and simmer for 20-25 minutes. Meanwhile, heat oil in a medium sauté pan over medium heat. Add carrots and cook 2 minutes. Add scallions, garlic, and ginger. Sauté 3 minutes more and set aside. When rice is cooked, stir in carrot mixture, soy sauce, and coriander.

Yield: 4 servings

BAKED SPICY RICE

1	cup long-grain rice, uncooked
2	(10-ounce) cans diced tomatoes and green chilis, undrained
1	cup water
1	teaspoon salt
⅔	cup pimiento-stuffed olives, sliced
¼	cup vegetable oil
½	cup chopped onion
1	cup shredded Monterey Jack cheese

Preheat oven to 350°. Combine all ingredients in a shallow 2-quart baking dish. Bake, covered, for 45 minutes. Stir well and continue baking, uncovered, 15 additional minutes or until liquid is absorbed and rice is tender.

Yield: 6-8 servings

SPICED RICE PILAF

4	tablespoons butter
½	cup finely chopped onion
I	teaspoon finely minced garlic
I½	cups white rice
I	tablespoon toasted mustard seeds
2¾	cups chicken stock
½	teaspoon salt
½	teaspoon curry powder

In a medium saucepan over medium heat, melt the butter. Add the onion and garlic and cook until soft but not colored. Add the rice and mustard seeds and stir for 1-2 minutes. Add the stock, salt, and curry. Bring to a boil and cover tightly. Reduce heat to a simmer and cook for 25 minutes. Remove from heat and let rice stand, covered, for 10 minutes. Fluff lightly with a fork and serve.

Yield: 4-6 servings

SPINACH FETA RICE

I	cup basmati brown rice
2¼	cups chicken broth
I	medium onion, chopped
I	cup sliced fresh mushrooms
2	cloves garlic, minced
	Vegetable cooking spray
I	tablespoon lemon juice
½	teaspoon dried oregano leaves
6	cups shredded fresh spinach
4	ounces feta cheese, crumbled
	Freshly ground black pepper

Combine rice and broth in saucepan. Bring to a boil and stir. Reduce heat, cover, and simmer for 45 minutes or until broth is absorbed. Cook onion, mushrooms, and garlic in oil-sprayed skillet until tender. Stir in lemon juice and oregano. Add spinach, cheese, and pepper to rice; toss until spinach is wilted.

Yield: 6 servings

134

SPICED CRANBERRY AND ORANGE RELISH

1⅓ cups sugar
⅔ cup water
2 small navel oranges
2½ cups fresh or frozen cranberries (thawed if frozen)
¼ teaspoon ground cinnamon
¼ teaspoon ground cloves
2 tablespoons minced drained stem ginger in syrup (not pickled) or crystallized ginger

Bring sugar and water to a boil in a 1½-quart heavy saucepan, stirring until sugar is dissolved. Reduce heat and simmer syrup for 5 minutes without stirring, washing down any sugar crystals on side of pan with a pastry brush dipped in cold water. While syrup simmers, cut oranges, including peel and pith, into 1-inch pieces, discarding any seeds, and combine with cranberries, cinnamon, and cloves in a food processor. Add sugar syrup and pulse until fruit is finely chopped. Transfer relish to a bowl and stir in ginger. Chill, covered, for 1 day for flavors to develop.

Cook's Note: *Relish can be chilled up to 1 week.*

Yield: 4 cups

That's one of the nicest things people say to me: "You make such happy art." It's not intentional; I'm a positive person.

FRUIT AND NUT TABOULI

- 1 cup bulgur
- 2¼ cups boiling water
- 2 seedless oranges
- ¼ cup lemon juice
- ¼ cup olive oil
- 1 clove garlic, minced
- ½ cup minced red onion
- ½ cucumber, peeled, seeded, and chopped
- 1½ cups chopped flat leaf parsley
- ½ cup chopped mint
- ¼ cup chopped walnuts, toasted
- ¼ cup golden raisins
- ½ teaspoon salt
- Freshly ground black pepper, to taste

Put bulgur in a medium bowl. Pour the boiling water over it. Cover the bowl with a plate and let the bulgur sit for 20 minutes. Drain it with a fine mesh strainer. Section the oranges with a paring knife. Cut away the peel and pith, and cut out the sections, leaving the membranes. Cut the sections in half and add them to the bulgur. Add the lemon juice, olive oil, garlic, onion, cucumber, parsley, mint, walnuts, and raisins, mixing well. Season with salt and pepper. Serve the tabouli at room temperature.

Yield: 6 servings

GRILLED BALSAMIC-GLAZED PEACHES

- ½   cup balsamic vinegar
- 3   tablespoons brown sugar
- 1   teaspoon cracked black pepper
- ⅛   teaspoon salt
- 6   firm, ripe peaches, halved
- ¼   cup vegetable oil

Combine vinegar, brown sugar, pepper, and salt in a saucepan and bring to a boil. Reduce heat and simmer 2-3 minutes. Place peaches in a shallow dish. Pour vinegar mixture over the peaches, tossing gently to coat. Let stand 10 minutes. Remove peaches from vinegar mixture, reserving 2 tablespoons of the mixture. Set aside remaining vinegar mixture. Whisk together reserved 2 tablespoons vinegar mixture and oil, blending well. Set vinaigrette aside. Place peach halves, cut sides down, on a lightly greased grill rack. Grill, covered with grill lid, over medium heat (300°-350°) for 5 minutes on each side or until firm and golden, basting with remaining vinegar mixture. Serve peaches with vinaigrette.

Cook's Note: *May also be baked at 350° in the oven. Serve this with grilled chicken, pork chops, or any grilled fish.*

Yield: 6 servings

Here's my darkest painting. I was sick one Christmas. Do you remember Robert Lewis Stevenson's poem "The Counterpane" about a child who was sick in bed all the time and there was a window counterpane and how he had all sorts of little soldiers? My mother would do the same for me and give me this little world that I could live with when I was sick and I used to love being sick. When I was sick that Christmas with the flu or something, I was alone and I started thinking about those days and I went into this sort of dream world, thinking about creative ideas and stories…

Entrées

ENTRÉES

CHESAPEAKE BAY BROILED FLOUNDER

4	whole dressed flounder (about 3 pounds)
1	teaspoon black pepper
2	tablespoons olive oil
3	tablespoons prepared brown mustard
2	tablespoons scallions, chopped as garnish
1	lime sliced as garnish

Preheat broiler. Arrange flounder on a baking sheet and sprinkle with pepper and olive oil. Spread prepared brown mustard evenly over the fish. Broil about 4 inches from the heat source for 5-8 minutes, or until golden brown, but do not overcook. Garnish with scallions and sliced lime.

Yield: 4 servings

The best:
Santa Marguerita
Pinot Grigio; the
frugal alternative:
Hugues Beaulieu
Picpoul de Pinet.

TILAPIA IN WHITE WINE SAUCE

4	(6-ounce) tilapia fillets
2	tablespoons butter
½	cup white wine
1	teaspoon lemon-pepper seasoning

Wash tilapia and place in a porcelain or oven proof dish. Melt butter in a pan, add wine cooking for 1 minute. Pour over fish and sprinkle with the seasoning. Cover and place in refrigerator for 2 hours. Preheat oven to 400°. Uncover and place tilapia in the oven and bake for 6 minutes or until done. Drizzle with a little of the sauce and serve immediately.

Yield: 4 servings

The best: Kunde
Sauvignon
Blanc: the frugal
alternative:
Snoqualamie
Sauvignon Blanc.

138

ROASTED FLOUNDER WITH OREGANO AND BAY

Extra virgin olive oil
6   lemons
24 dried bay leaves
¼   cup dried wild oregano
6   whole dressed flounder,
    (12 to 14 ounces each)
    Coarse sea salt and coarsely ground black
    pepper
1   teaspoon capers, drained

The best: Santa Marguerita Pinot Grigio. The frugal alternative: Hugues Beaulieu Picpoul de Pinet.

Preheat oven to 450°. Brush shallow baking pans with olive oil. Slice 2 of the lemons into fine rounds ⅛-inch thick. Scatter half the bay leaves, a few of the lemon slices, and some oregano on the bottom of the pans. Place the fish on top, season generously with salt and pepper, then scatter the remaining dried oregano, bay leaves, and lemon slices on top of the fish to cover them. Drizzle generously with olive oil and bake for 15-20 minutes. When cooked, remove the flounder from the baking pans, and place on serving plates. Place the baking pans with remaining herbs and fish juices over medium heat and deglaze with the juice from the 3 remaining lemons, adding capers. Serve each flounder with some of the sauce from the pans, the herb leaves, and lemon wedges.

Yield: 6 servings

GRILLED TUNA WITH WASABI-LIME BUTTER

4	(6-ounce) fresh tuna steaks, sushimi grade, about ¾-inch thick
	Vegetable oil
3	teaspoons minced fresh dill weed
	Cracked black pepper
6	tablespoons cold butter
3	scallions, finely sliced
1	teaspoon minced fresh cilantro
1½	tablespoons fresh lime juice
3	tablespoons soy sauce
	Black pepper
1-1½	tablespoons prepared wasabi or to taste

Brush tuna steaks lightly on both sides with oil. Sprinkle dill weed and pepper to season. Marinate 20 minutes while heating grill. Assemble sauce ingredients. In a small, heavy skillet place the cold butter, scallions, cilantro, lime juice, soy sauce, pepper, and wasabi. Place tuna steaks on the grill and sear 3 minutes. Turn and grill 1½ to 2 minutes until tuna is nicely marked on outside, and rare inside. Do not overcook. While, tuna is cooking, heat sauce ingredients over medium heat, whisking constantly until butter melts and sauce is emulsified and warm, about 2 minutes. Place grilled tuna steaks on warm plates. Divide sauce over top of each portion.

Yield: 4 servings

The best: Ojai Pisoni Vineyards; the frugal alternative: Smoking Loon Pinot Noir.

140

SAUTÉED RED SNAPPER WITH ROASTED TOMATOES

The best: Testarossa
Pinot Noir; the frugal
alternative: Finca
Sobreno Crianza.

3	ripe tomatoes, about 2½ inches in diameter; or 5-6 large plum tomatoes
	Salt and freshly ground black pepper to taste
½	teaspoon dried oregano
½	teaspoon dried basil
	Olive oil
2	teaspoons soy sauce
1	medium clove garlic, finely chopped
1½	tablespoons freshly squeezed lemon juice
4	(7-ounce) snapper fillets
1	tablespoon vegetable oil
	Salt and black pepper to taste
	Flour for dredging

Preheat oven to 550°. Place the rack at the top. Rinse and dry the tomatoes, cut out and discard the core, and cut each regular tomato into 4-6 wedges. If using plum tomatoes, cut them in half lengthwise. Put the tomatoes in a mixing bowl and season with salt, pepper, oregano, and basil. Lightly oil a large roasting pan and immediately pour the tomatoes with any juices into it, or place the plum tomatoes cut side down with any juices. Roast the tomatoes on the top rack until they're soft and squishy and the skins are blistered, 10-15 minutes. Reduce the oven temperature to 400°, and lower the rack to the middle. Scrape the tomatoes out of the roasting pan onto cutting board and chop them into medium pieces. Remove and discard the skins. Put the chopped tomatoes into a mixing bowl. Put the soy sauce into the roasting pan and scrape up any brown bits. Add the soy sauce and brown bits to the chopped tomato along with the garlic and lemon juice. Season the mixture well with salt and pepper and set aside. (This can be made up to 3 days ahead and kept refrigerated.) Season the snapper fillets with salt and pepper. Place 1 or 2 large ovenproof skillets over high heat with the vegetable oil. (If using 2 pans, divide the oil equally between them.) Meanwhile, dredge the fillets lightly in flour and pat off the excess. When the oil is hot, place the fillets in the skillet(s), skin side up, for about 3 minutes, or until lightly golden brown.

Turn the fillets over and place the skillet(s) in the oven. Roast the fillets until they are just cooked through, about 5 minutes. To serve, place the snapper fillets on warm dinner plates and spoon some of the warmed or room temperature roasted tomatoes next to each.

Cook's Note: *The sauce is simple but has a complex flavor, complimenting the fish beautifully. Salmon, bass, catfish, or sole may also be used.*

Yield: 4 servings

Both of these suggestions are dry, full-bodied Rieslings. The best: Hans Lang Riesling Trocken; the frugal alternative: Waipara Hills Dry Riesling.

BASS WITH
PICO DE GALLO SALSA

1	pound plum tomatoes, diced
⅓	cup diced red onion
⅓	cup chopped black olives
2	tablespoons chopped fresh cilantro
2	tablespoons seeded and chopped jalapeño
½-1	tablespoon fresh lime juice
	Freshly ground black pepper to taste
	Hot pepper sauce to taste
1	teaspoon minced garlic
2-3	tablespoons olive oil, divided
2	pounds bass fillets

Prepare grill or preheat oven to 425°. Mix together tomatoes, onion, olives, cilantro, jalapeño, lime juice, pepper, a dash of hot sauce, garlic, and 2 tablespoons olive oil in a nonreactive bowl. Adjust seasoning with additional lime juice and pepper if necessary. Oil the bass fillets and either grill or bake them for 12-15 minutes. Cut into serving pieces and top each serving with 2 spoonsful of the sauce.

Cook's Note: *Swordfish or halibut may also be used.*

Yield: 4 servings

142

COD WITH OLIVE TAPENADE

¼	cup chopped Kalamata olives
¼	cup chopped Spanish olives
2	teaspoons capers
2-3	teaspoons minced garlic
1½	tablespoons olive oil, divided
1	tablespoon balsamic vinegar
⅓	cup diced tomatoes
2	tablespoons minced fresh parsley, optional
	Salt and freshly ground black pepper to taste
1½-2	pounds cod fillets

Preheat the broiler. Mix together the olives, capers, garlic, one tablespoon of the olive oil, vinegar, tomatoes, and parsley, if using, in a medium nonreactive bowl. Season with salt and pepper. Set aside while preparing the cod. Coat the fillets on both sides with the remaining olive oil. Place in a broiling pan, broil for 8-10 minutes, or until cooked through. It is unnecessary to turn the fish—the heat of the pan will cook the bottom side. Remove from the pan and spoon the olive mixture over the fillets.

Cook's Note: *Any mild flavored fish may be used.*

Yield: 4 servings

GRILLED SNAPPER WITH ORANGE BUTTER

6	(6-ounce) snapper or grouper fillets
2	tablespoons olive oil
1	teaspoon sea salt
1	teaspoon freshly ground black pepper
1	teaspoon thyme, chopped
½	cup butter
½	cup sliced almonds
2	teaspoons orange zest

Rub the fish with a mixture of olive oil, salt, pepper, and thyme. Grill for 4-5 minutes per side until fish flakes. Melt butter in pan. Add almonds and zest and sauté for 3-4 minutes to slightly brown almonds. Spoon over fish and serve immediately.

Yield: 6 servings

BLUEFISH WITH MUSTARD SAUCE

1   cup mayonnaise
⅓   cup Dijon mustard
¼   cup bottled horseradish
¼   cup minced onion
¼   cup finely chopped fresh parsley
     Worcestershire sauce to taste
     Hot pepper sauce to taste
     Olive oil
2   pounds bluefish fillets

Preheat the broiler. Combine mayonnaise, mustard, horseradish, onion, parsley, and a generous dash of Worcestershire and hot pepper sauces in a medium bowl. Set aside. Lightly oil the fillets and place in a broiler pan. Broil until almost done. Remove the fillets, spread lightly with the sauce, and return to the broiler until the topping is lightly browned, 2-3 minutes.

Cook's Note: Grilled tuna, salmon, mahi-mahi or grouper may also be used with this sauce.

Yield: 4 servings

Hot sauce and horseradish call for a relatively sweet, full-bodied wine such as Schumann-Nagler Christopher Philip Rheingau Riesling.

PEPPER CRUSTED SALMON

2	tablespoons soy sauce
1	clove garlic, minced
2	teaspoons fresh lemon juice
1	teaspoon granulated sugar
2	(6-ounce) salmon fillets, skinned and halved
4	teaspoons coarsely ground black pepper
2	tablespoons olive oil

In a zip-lock bag combine the soy sauce, garlic, lemon juice, and sugar. Add the salmon, coating it well, and marinate, chilled for 30 minutes. Remove salmon from the bag, discarding the marinade, pat it dry and press 2 teaspoons of black pepper onto each piece of salmon, coating thoroughly. In a heavy skillet heat the olive oil over moderately high heat until it is hot but not smoking and sauté the salmon for 2 minutes on each side, or until it just flakes. Transfer salmon with a slotted spoon to paper towels and let it drain for 30 seconds.

Yield: 2 servings

SALMON WITH THYME AND MUSTARD SAUCE

½	cup "country style" Dijon mustard
4½	tablespoons pure maple syrup, divided
3½	tablespoons water
2	tablespoons horseradish
6	(6-ounce) salmon fillets
1½	tablespoons light brown sugar
1½	tablespoons chopped fresh thyme

Preheat oven to 350°. Whisk mustard, 3 tablespoons syrup, water, and horseradish together and spread over fillets. Bake 14 minutes. Blend remaining syrup, brown sugar, and thyme and spoon over fish. May be served hot or cold.

Yield: 6 servings

Australian Shiraz is known for its cracked black pepper nose. The nose comes from the vines when they have been under stress. The best: Gemtree Uncut Shiraz; the frugal alternative: Milton Park Shiraz.

This dish is sweet and hot, pair with a Riesling. The best: Winzer von Erbach Riesling; the frugal alternative: Erbacher Honigberg Riesling.

POACHED SALMON WITH HERBED AÏOLI

1	small onion, sliced
1	medium carrot, chopped
1	stalk celery, chopped
6	whole black peppercorns
1	whole bay leaf
½	cup dry white wine
	Water
4	(6-ounce) salmon fillets
	Salt and white pepper
½	cup mayonnaise
½	cup flat leaf parsley, chopped
1	scallion, chopped
1	tablespoon fresh tarragon, chopped
1	teaspoon white wine vinegar
1	clove garlic, chopped

The best: Louis Jadot Chassagne Montrachet "Morgeot" Clos de la Chapelle Duc de Magent Premier Cru; the frugal alternative: Saint Helen Ranch Chardonnay.

In a medium skillet combine onion, carrot, celery, peppercorns, bay leaf, and wine. Add enough water to come 1½-inches up the side of skillet. Bring to a boil, reduce heat and simmer 15 minutes. Season fillets with salt and pepper and place in the skillet. Cover and simmer 5 minutes. Remove from heat and let stand until fillets are opaque, 8-10 minutes. While the salmon is cooking, combine mayonnaise, parsley, scallion, tarragon, vinegar, and garlic in a food processor and process until smooth and creamy. Serve salmon with a dollop of sauce on each fillet.

Yield: 4 servings

GENTLEMEN, YOU ARE WELCOME

DRINK WHAT YOU PLEASE

SIT DOWN AT YOUR EASE

PAY WHAT YOU CALL FOR

HERBED SALMON WITH SOUTHWEST BEANS

The heartiness of this dish, and the pepper, call for a Pinot Noir. The best: Byron Nielson Vineyard Pinot Noir; the frugal alternative: Finca Sobreno Toro Crianza.

SOUTHWEST BEANS

1	tablespoon corn oil
½	onion, diced
¼	cup celery, diced
½	green bell pepper, diced
1	tablespoon jalapeño pepper, seeded, minced
2	cloves garlic, minced
1	teaspoon ground cumin
1	(14-ounce) can cannelloni beans, rinsed and drained
1	plum tomato, cored and diced
1¼	cups chicken broth or water
1	tablespoon red wine vinegar
2	tablespoons cilantro, chopped
	Salt and freshly ground black pepper to taste

SALMON AND MARINADE

3	pounds salmon fillets or steaks
3	tablespoons lime juice
2	tablespoons olive oil
2	tablespoons parsley, chopped
2	tablespoons chives, chopped
1	teaspoon thyme, chopped
1	teaspoon black peppercorns, crushed

To prepare bean stew, heat oil, add onions, celery, pepper, jalapeño, and garlic. Sauté over medium-high heat about 3 minutes. Add cumin and sauté another 30 seconds. Add beans, tomato, and enough broth to just cover the beans, cooking 20 minutes. Stir frequently. While stew is cooking, marinate fish. Combine marinade ingredients in a zip-lock bag, add salmon, seal, and marinate 15 minutes. Thicken the stew, using back of wooden spoon to mash some of the beans. Add vinegar and simmer until vinegar's raw taste dissipates, about 2 minutes. Stir in cilantro just before serving. Season with salt and pepper. Preheat grill. Remove salmon from marinade and grill about 2-3 minutes per side. Serve with stew.

Yield: 6 servings

SCALLOP AND ASPARAGUS RISOTTO

4	cups chicken broth
¼	cup olive oil, divided
1	cup onion, finely chopped
2	cups Arborio rice, uncooked
2	cups white wine
¼	teaspoon freshly ground black pepper
2	tablespoons butter
½	cup Asiago cheese, grated
24	asparagus spears, cut diagonally into 1-inch pieces
2½	pounds sea scallops, muscle tabs removed
	Salt and white pepper to taste

Bring broth to a boil in a medium saucepan. Reduce heat and simmer. Heat 2 tablespoons oil in a large saucepan. Add onion; reduce heat and sauté 1 minute. Add rice and cook, stirring to coat, about 2 minutes. Add half of the simmered chicken broth to rice and cook, stirring constantly, until the rice absorbs all the broth, about 6-8 minutes. Add remaining broth and simmer, stirring, until broth is absorbed, 6-8 minutes. Add wine and simmer, stirring, until risotto has a creamy consistency and rice is tender, about 6-8 minutes. Stir in pepper, butter, and cheese in the final minutes of cooking. Steam asparagus until tender, about 4 minutes. Set aside. Pat scallops dry with paper toweling and season with salt and pepper. Sauté scallops in the remaining olive oil over very high heat until they are golden brown, about 2 minutes per side. When scallops are done, serve them at once on a bed of risotto. Top with the asparagus.

Yield: 8 servings

The best: Matanzas Creek Sauvignon Blanc; the frugal alternative: Domaine Loyer Bastie Sauvignon Blanc.

SOY CITRUS SCALLOPS

- ⅔ cup soy sauce
- ¼ cup freshly squeezed lemon juice
- ¼ cup freshly squeezed lime juice
- 3 tablespoons plus 1 teaspoon granulated sugar
- 3 teaspoons finely grated peeled fresh ginger
- 2 teaspoons Asian sesame oil
- 2 pounds large sea scallops (about 30), tough muscle removed
- 2 teaspoons vegetable oil
  Sesame seeds, toasted

The best: Matanzas Creek Sauvignon Blanc; the frugal alternative: Domaine Loyer Bastie Sauvignon Blanc.

Whisk together soy sauce, lemon and lime juices, sugar, ginger, and sesame oil in a wide shallow nonreactive bowl. Add scallops and marinate, covered at room temperature, 5 minutes on each side (do not marinate any longer, or scallops will become mushy once cooked). Transfer scallops to a plate reserving marinade. Heat ½ teaspoon vegetable oil in a 12-inch nonstick skillet over moderately high heat until hot but not smoking, then sauté scallops, 6-8 at a time, turning once, until golden brown and just cooked through, 4-6 minutes total, transferring to a plate as cooked. Wipe out skillet and add ½ teaspoon oil between batches. Wipe out skillet again, then add marinade and boil until reduced to about ⅓ cup, about 2 minutes. Drizzle scallops with sauce and sprinkle with sesame seeds.

Yield: 6 servings

I love crab. Finding a good crab cake is my goal in life.

MUSSELS WITH PARSLEY AND GARLIC

- 2 pounds mussels, cleaned and beards removed
- 3 cloves garlic, coarsely chopped
- 1 cup fresh flat leaf parsley
- 4 tablespoons butter, cut into pieces
  Coarse salt
- ¼ teaspoon freshly ground black pepper
- 2 tablespoons white wine

Preheat oven to 450°. Spread mussels in a 13x9-inch baking dish. Blend all remaining ingredients to a paste in a food processor. Spoon mixture over mussels. Cover tightly with foil and bake in middle of oven until all mussels are open, 12-15 minutes. Discard any unopened mussels.

Yield: 4 servings

Meinklang Blanc de Noir Frizzante is a slightly fizzy, slightly pink wine made from Pinot Noir that will stand up to the garlic.

CHESAPEAKE BAY CRAB CAKES

- 3 crackers (Ritz or soda crackers), crushed
- ½ cup light mayonnaise
- 1 package Old Bay Crab Cake seasoning
- 1 large egg
- 1 pound lump or backfin crabmeat
- 3 tablespoons peanut oil

Mix together crackers, mayonnaise, Old Bay, and egg. Add crab, tossing gently, not breaking up crabmeat. Shape into 4-6 crab cakes and pan fry in oil until golden brown and firm and heated through. May broil 3-4 minutes per side.

Yield: 4-6 servings

The best German Riesling Kabinett that you can afford; a Mosel would be best, but any will do. The best: Gessinger Zeltinger Sonnenuhr Riesling Kabinett; the frugal alternative: Covey Run Riesling.

CRABMEAT IN SCALLOP SHELLS

- 1 medium onion, chopped
- 4 tablespoons butter, divided
- 8 ounces mushrooms, sliced
- 1½ tablespoons dry Sherry
  Dash nutmeg
  Salt and white pepper
- 2 pounds lump crabmeat
- 8 ounces shredded white Cheddar cheese
  Parmesan-Reggiano cheese
- 2 tablespoons to ½ cup dry breadcrumbs

SAUCE
- 3 tablespoons butter, melted
- 4½ tablespoons all-purpose flour
- ¼ teaspoons salt
  Dash of black pepper
  Dash of red pepper
- 1½ cups chicken broth
- ½ cup half-and-half

Preheat oven to 350°. In a skillet, sauté onion in 2 tablespoons melted butter until transparent. Place in bowl and set aside. Sauté mushrooms over medium heat in 2 tablespoons melted butter about 5 minutes. Add Sherry. Cook until some of the liquid is absorbed, about 5 minutes. Add dash of nutmeg, salt, and pepper to taste. Set aside. For the sauce, melt butter, stir in flour, salt, and both peppers; blending well. Add chicken broth, continue stirring until thickened. Bring gradually to a boil for 2 minutes. Add half-and-half slowly. Allow to cool. Mix crabmeat, mushrooms, sautéed onions, and Cheddar cheese with sauce. Place in 8 scallop shells or ramekins. Top with Parmesan cheese and dried breadcrumbs. Bake for 20-30 minutes or until brown and bubbly.

Cook's Note: *Crabmeat mixture may be prepared and refrigerated before ready to cook.*

Yield: 8 servings

Mushrooms, butter, Cheddar, and Parmesan-Reggiano call for a big, buttery Chardonnay, such as: Sonoma-Cutrer Russian River Ranches.

SHRIMP FETA WITH ORZO

1   medium onion, finely chopped
3   cloves garlic, minced
½   teaspoon dried oregano, crumbled
¼   teaspoon dried hot red pepper flakes
2   tablespoons olive oil, divided
½   cup dry white wine
1   (28-ounce) can crushed tomatoes
1   teaspoon salt
1½ pounds large shrimp, shelled and deveined
1   pound orzo
½   cup Kalamata or other brine-cured black
    olives pitted and chopped
    Salt and black pepper to taste
1   pound feta cheese, patted dry, crumbled,
    and divided

Santorini Dry White Wine naturally enhances the Athenian flavors.

Preheat oven to 425°. Cook onion, garlic, oregano, and red pepper flakes in 1 tablespoon oil in a 4-quart heavy pot over moderately high heat, stirring, until onion is softened, about 3 minutes. Add wine and boil until reduced by ½, about 3 minutes. Stir in tomatoes and salt, then reduce heat, and simmer briskly, stirring frequently, until slightly thickened, about 8 minutes. Stir shrimp into sauce and simmer, stirring occasionally, until shrimp are just cooked through, about 3 minutes. While sauce and shrimp are cooking, cook orzo in a 6-quart pot of boiling salted water until al dente. Reserve ½ cup cooking water, and drain orzo in a sieve. Return orzo to pot and toss with remaining tablespoon oil. Stir in sauce with shrimp and reserved cooking water, add olives, salt, and pepper. Spoon ½ of pasta into an oiled 13x9x2-inch glass-baking dish, and sprinkle with ½ of feta. Top with remaining pasta and feta, and bake in middle of oven, uncovered, until cheese is slightly melted and pasta is heated through, 10-15 minutes.

Yield: 6 servings

152

GRILLED HERBED SHRIMP WITH MANGO SALSA

SHRIMP

- 3 cloves garlic, minced
- 1 medium yellow onion, small-diced
- 1/4 cup minced fresh parsley
- 1/4 cup minced fresh basil
- 1 teaspoon dry mustard
- 2 teaspoons Dijon mustard
- 1 teaspoon Kosher salt
- 1/4 teaspoon freshly ground black pepper
- 1/4 cup extra virgin olive oil
  Juice of 1 lemon
- 2 pounds jumbo shrimp (16 to 20 per pound) peeled (tails left on) and deveined

MANGO SALSA

- 2 tablespoons olive oil
- 1 1/2 cups diced yellow onion
- 2 teaspoons peeled, minced fresh ginger
- 1 1/2 teaspoons minced garlic
- 2 ripe mangoes, peeled, seeded, and small-diced
- 1/3 cup freshly squeezed orange juice
- 2 teaspoons light brown sugar
- 1/2 teaspoon Kosher salt
- 1/2 teaspoon freshly ground black pepper
- 1-2 teaspoons minced fresh jalapeño pepper, seeded, to taste
- 2 teaspoons minced fresh mint leaves

J.B. Adam
Gewürztraminer
pairs well with spicy,
fruity salsa.

Combine the garlic, onion, parsley, basil, mustards, salt, pepper, olive oil, and lemon juice. Add the shrimp and allow to marinate for 1 hour at room temperature or cover and refrigerate for up to 2 days. Prepare a charcoal grill with hot coals, brushing the grill rack with oil to prevent the shrimp from sticking. Skewer the shrimp using 5 or 6 shrimp on a 12-inch skewer for a dinner serving. Grill shrimp for 1 1/2 minutes on each side. To prepare salsa, sauté the olive oil, onion, and ginger in a large sauté pan over medium-low heat for

10 minutes, or until the onions are translucent. Add the garlic and cook for 1 more minute. Add mangoes; reduce the heat to low and cook for 10 more minutes. Add orange juice, sugar, salt, pepper, and jalapeños; cook for 10 more minutes, or until the orange juice is reduced, stirring occasionally. Remove from heat and add mint. Serve with grilled shrimp.

Yield: 6 servings

SHRIMP AND PEPPER KABOBS

1	pound shrimp, peeled with tails left on
1	cup lemon juice
¾	cup vegetable oil
½	cup soy sauce
⅓	cup chopped, fresh parsley
⅓	cup finely chopped onion
1	teaspoon salt
1	teaspoon black pepper
2	cloves garlic, minced
2	medium-size green bell peppers, seeded and cut into pieces
2	medium-size sweet red bell peppers, seeded and cut into pieces
2	cups hot cooked rice

The best: J.B.Adam Gewürztraminer; the frugal alternative: Covey Run Gewürztraminer.

Arrange shrimp in a large shallow dish. Combine lemon juice, oil, soy sauce, parsley, onion, salt, pepper, and garlic in a medium bowl; stir well. Pour half of mixture over shrimp. Cover and marinate in refrigerator 4 hours. Drain shrimp, discarding marinade. Thread shrimp onto four 12-inch skewers alternately with pepper pieces. Grill over medium coals 3-4 minutes on each side or until shrimp turn pink, basting with remaining half of marinade mixture. Serve kabobs over hot cooked rice.

Yield: 4 servings

LIME GARLIC SHRIMP

2 pounds medium shrimp, cleaned, peeled, deveined
¼ cup butter or margarine
4 cloves garlic, minced
I cup scallions, minced
¼ cup fresh squeezed lime juice
Coarsely ground black pepper, to taste
Hot sauce, to taste
¼ cup freshly chopped parsley
Cooked rice

Prepare shrimp and set aside. In a large sauté pan, melt the butter or margarine. Add garlic and scallions and cook until the scallions turn bright green. Add shrimp and lime juice. Cook until shrimp turn pink. Add the pepper, hot sauce, and parsley. Serve over rice.

Cook's Note: *This easy to fix shrimp dish is great when accompanied by a citrus salad.*

Yield: 4 servings

Covey Run Gewürztraminer enhances the tangy lime sauce.

The best: Kennedy Point Sauvignon Blanc; the frugal alternative: Firefinch Sauvignon Blanc.

TUNA MARINADE

¼ cup peanut oil
2 tablespoons dry Sherry
3 tablespoons soy sauce
½ teaspoon dried ground ginger

Whisk all ingredients together. Marinate tuna steaks, salmon or mahi-mahi for 6-8 hours in refrigerator and grill selected fish.

Yield: ½ cup

SOUTHWEST MARINADE

¼	cup olive oil
1	teaspoon grated lime zest
¼	cup lime juice
4	teaspoons Worcestershire sauce
1½	teaspoons ground cumin
2	cloves garlic, minced
¼	teaspoon each salt and black pepper

Whisk ingredients together and use as a marinade for salmon or any firm fish.

Yield: ¾ cup

The best: Adelsheim Pinot Noir; the frugal alternative: Panarroz Jumilla Red Wine.

CUCUMBER SOUR CREAM SAUCE

1	cup (packed) baby spinach leaves
1	cup (packed) arugula leaves
2	scallions, finely chopped
¾	cup sour cream
3	tablespoons whole grain Dijon mustard
½	cup chopped, seeded, peeled cucumber
	Salt and white pepper

Finely chop spinach, arugula, and scallions in a food processor. Add sour cream and mustard; process until just blended. Transfer to medium bowl. Stir cucumber into sour cream mixture. Season to taste with salt and pepper. Excellent served with salmon, halibut or snapper.

Yield: 2 cups

Nothing goes with cream sauce like an Amontillado, and Emilio Lustau makes the best.

LEMON CAPER SAUCE

- ¼ cup mayonnaise
- 1 teaspoon Dijon mustard
- ¼ teaspoon hot pepper sauce
- ½ teaspoon lemon juice
- 1 teaspoon drained, chopped capers
- ½ teaspoon finely chopped onion
- 1 teaspoon finely chopped dill
- 1 teaspoon finely chopped dill pickle or cornichons

  Lemon

Mix all ingredients. Set aside in refrigerator until ready to serve. Serve with any grilled or baked fish. Garnish with a wedge of lemon, if desired.

Yield: ¼ cup

Kennedy Point Sauvignon Blanc nicely stands up to this pungent sauce.

BALSAMIC DRIZZLE

- 1 cup balsamic vinegar
- ⅓ cup honey
- ⅓ cup granulated sugar
- 3 tablespoons soy sauce

Place all ingredients in a large, heavy, nonreactive saucepan over medium heat and bring to a boil. Simmer the mixture until reduced to 1 cup, about 15 minutes. Skim off and discard any foam that may rise to the surface. Strain the mixture into a bottle and cool to room temperature. Cork or cap the bottle, and refrigerate.

Cook's Note: *This will keep for several months. Good served on any fish or grilled vegetables.*

Yield: 1 cup

Avignonesi Rosso Toscano is an excellent pairing for this full bodied sauce.

FRICASSEED CHICKEN WITH GRAPE TOMATOES AND OLIVES

- 3½ pound chicken, cut into 8 pieces
- 1 tablespoon extra virgin olive oil
- 4-5 cloves garlic, peeled
- 2 teaspoons rosemary leaves, finely chopped
  Salt
- ¼ teaspoon chopped hot chili pepper, or to taste
- ½ cup dry white wine
- 24 grape tomatoes
- 12 small black olives in brine such as Italian Riviera or French Niçoise olives

Bruno Franco Roero Arneis is an Italian white which compliments the Mediterranean flavors.

Wash all the chicken pieces in cold water and pat dry. Choose a skillet or sauté pan that can contain all the chicken pieces in one layer without crowding. Put in the oil, garlic, and rosemary and turn on the heat to high. Add the chicken, browning both sides. Sprinkle with salt, add the chili pepper, and baste with liquid in pan. Add the wine and scrape up any browning residues sticking to the bottom of the pan. Put a lid on the pan and turn the heat down to low. Cook about 35 minutes, turning the chicken over from time to time, adding 2 -3 tablespoons of water if too dry. When the chicken is very tender, the meat should come easily off the bone; add the tomatoes and olives. Continue cooking just until the tomatoes' skins begin to crack.

Cook's Note: The chicken can be cooked several hours in advance to the point before adding tomatoes and olives. Reheat on low and add tomatoes and olives after chicken is thoroughly reheated.

Yield: 4 servings

CHICKEN PICCATA WITH MUSHROOMS AND CAPERS

4	skinless boneless chicken breast halves
	Salt and black pepper to taste
1	tablespoon all-purpose flour
2	tablespoons olive oil
2	tablespoons butter
½	pound mushrooms, sliced
½	cup dry white wine
¼	cup fresh lemon juice
3	tablespoons capers
4	tablespoons grated Parmesan cheese
	Lemon, thinly sliced for garnish

Rosés get a bad rap because of White Zinfandel, but a dry Rosé like Château Routas from Provence, or Margan Shiraz Saignée from Australia will stand up to the capers like no white wine will.

Place chicken breasts between 2 sheets of waxed paper and pound chicken to ¼-inch thickness. Sprinkle with salt, pepper, and flour. Brown on both sides in olive oil. Remove and keep warm. Add butter to skillet and sauté mushrooms until tender. Remove mushrooms with slotted spoon and set aside. Add white wine and lemon juice to skillet. Deglaze pan and simmer a few minutes, scraping up any brown bits in pan. Add capers and Parmesan cheese. Return chicken and mushrooms to skillet and simmer 2 minutes. Turn and continue to simmer 1-2 minutes more to heat through. To serve, place chicken on plates and spoon sauce over. Garnish with thin slices of lemon.

Yield: 4 servings

CHICKEN WITH GREEN OLIVES, ORANGE, AND SHERRY

2	tablespoons olive oil
1	(4-5-pound) chicken, cut into 8 pieces
	Salt and black pepper
1	cup sliced shallots, about 3 large
2	cloves garlic, minced
1	cup medium Sherry
1	cup low-salt chicken broth
1	orange, halved lengthwise, each half cut into 5 wedges
⅓	cup brine-cured green olives, pitted
1	tablespoon honey

Preheat oven to 425°. Heat oil in large ovenproof skillet over high heat. Sprinkle chicken with salt and pepper. Add chicken to skillet; cook until skin is crisp and browned, about 6 minutes per side. Transfer chicken to plate. Reduce heat to medium-high. Drain all but 2 tablespoons drippings from skillet. Add shallots; stir until soft and beginning to brown, about 2 minutes. Add garlic; stir 30 seconds. Add Sherry; boil until reduced by half, scraping up browned bits, about 3 minutes. Add chicken broth; bring to boil. Return chicken, skin side up, to skillet. Place orange wedges and olives among chicken pieces. Transfer to oven and braise uncovered until chicken is cooked through, about 20 minutes. Transfer chicken to platter. Bring sauce to boil over high heat. Stir in honey; boil until thickened, about 5 minutes. Check seasonings. Pour sauce, oranges, and olives over chicken, and return chicken to skillet and serve.

Yield: 4 servings

The best: Chalk Hill Cabernet Sauvignon; the frugal alternative: Dante Cabernet Sauvignon.

BALSAMIC CHICKEN WITH WILD MUSHROOMS

André Brunel Côtes du Rhône stands up to the full bodied sauce.

I	ounce dried Porcini mushrooms
6	chicken thighs, rinsed and patted dry
	Black pepper
	Flour for dredging
2	¼-inch thick slices of slab bacon, about ¼ pound, cut crosswise into ⅓-inch pieces
	Salt
I	tablespoon olive oil
3	cloves garlic, minced
½	cup fruity red wine, such as Beaujolais
½	cup beef broth
¼	cup balsamic vinegar, divided
I	teaspoon cornstarch dissolved in 2 teaspoons cold water
¾	cup drained and chopped prepared tomatoes
	Minced fresh flat-leafed parsley for garnish

In a small bowl soak the Porcini in I cup boiling water for 10 minutes, or until they are soft, drain well, reserving the liquid. Season chicken with pepper and dredge in flour, shaking off excess. In a large heavy skillet cook the bacon over moderate heat, stirring, until golden and crisp, transfer to paper towels and drain. Add the chicken to the skillet, skin side down, and cook turning occasionally for 20 minutes, until it is golden and crisp. Transfer chicken to a plate, season with salt, and discard fat in skillet. Add oil to skillet and cook garlic over low heat, stirring for I minute. Add reserved Porcini liquid, wine, broth, and 3 tablespoons of vinegar and boil mixture for 4 minutes. Add cornstarch mixture in a stream, stirring, stir in tomatoes, add chicken, turning to coat with sauce. Simmer the mixture, covered, for 10 minutes. Stir in remaining I tablespoon vinegar with salt and pepper, to taste. Garnish with parsley.

Yield: 6 servings

ROASTED LEMON CHICKEN

¾   cup butter, softened
2   teaspoons lemon zest
4   tablespoons lemon juice, divided
    Salt and white pepper, to taste
6   pounds roasting chicken

Preheat oven to 425°. In a bowl, cream together butter, lemon zest, 2 tablespoons lemon juice, drop by drop, and add salt and pepper to taste. Loosen the skin of chicken, rinsed and patted dry, by slipping fingers between skin and flesh, being careful not to pierce the skin, beginning at the neck and working down to and including tops of drumsticks. Spread half butter mixture under the skin and pat chicken to smooth butter into a uniform layer. Truss chicken and rub with remaining butter mixture. Arrange chicken, breast side down on an oiled rack in a baking pan and roast for 20 minutes. Turn chicken carefully, breast side up, sprinkle with remaining lemon juice, and roast, basting with pan juices, for 1 hour more, or until juices run clear when the fleshy part of the thigh is pricked with a skewer. Let chicken stand for 15 minutes before serving.

Yield: 6 servings

Butter and lemons equal Chardonnay every time. The best: Sonoma Cutrer Russian River Ranches; the frugal alternative: Milton Park Chardonnay.

NANCY THOMAS 2005

CHICKEN WITH PEARS AND STILTON

6	boneless, skinless chicken breast halves
	Flour for coating
6	tablespoons clarified butter, divided
	Salt and white pepper, to taste
¾	cup unsalted chicken stock
¾	cup Port
1½	cups heavy cream
3	pears, peeled, cored and cut into sixths, medium ripe
4	tablespoons Stilton cheese, divided
2	tablespoons minced, fresh parsley

A slightly sweeter red wine such as an Australian Shiraz. The best: Thorn-Clarke Shotfire Ridge; the frugal alternative: Step Road Blackwing Shiraz.

Preheat oven to 200°. Pound chicken breast to flatten slightly and sprinkle lightly with flour. Heat 4 tablespoons butter in skillet over moderately high heat. When butter begins to color slightly, add chicken. Cook 4 minutes, turn and continue cooking until chicken is springy to touch. Remove to warm platter. Sprinkle with salt and pepper, tent with foil and set in oven to keep warm. Add stock and Port to same skillet and boil until liquid is reduced by half. Add cream and boil until reduced to a sauce-like consistency. Place pears in another skillet and sauté for 5 minutes in the remaining 2 tablespoons butter. Set aside. Add 2 tablespoons Stilton to Port sauce and stir until melted. Place chicken on 6 serving plates and top each with 3 pear slices, some of the sauce, 1 teaspoon crumbled Stilton and 1 teaspoon parsley.

Yield: 6 servings

LEMON-GINGER GRILLED CHICKEN

4	tablespoons lemon zest
⅔	cup lemon juice
4	teaspoons ginger, peeled and minced
4	teaspoons light brown sugar, firmly packed
1	tablespoon vegetable oil
1	tablespoon salt or to taste
1	teaspoon crushed red pepper
3	pounds boneless, skinless chicken thighs or breasts

Combine the lemon zest, lemon juice, ginger, brown sugar, oil, salt, and crushed red pepper in a zip lock bag. Add the chicken, squeeze out the air, and seal the bag; turn to coat the chicken. Refrigerate, turning the bag occasionally, 15-30 minutes. Spray the grill or broiler rack with nonstick spray. Preheat the grill. Grill the chicken until cooked through, about 6 minutes per side. If broiling, position the rack about 5 inches from the heat source and preheat on high. Broil the chicken until cooked through, about 6 minutes.

Yield: 8 servings

Ca'del Solo Big House White enhances the citrus, spicy notes of the chicken.

CHICKEN FETTUCCINE SUPREME

The best: Fattoria Scopone Brunello di Montalcino; the frugal alternative: Scacciapensieri.

¼	cup butter or margarine
1¼	pounds skinless boneless chicken breast halves, cut into bite-size pieces
3	cups sliced fresh mushrooms
1	cup chopped scallions
1	small, sweet red bell pepper, cut into thin strips
1	clove garlic, crushed
½	teaspoon salt or to taste
½	teaspoon white pepper or to taste
10	ounces dried fettuccine, cooked
¾	cup half-and-half
¼	cup butter or margarine, melted
¼	cup chopped fresh parsley
¼	teaspoon salt
¼	teaspoon white pepper
½	cup grated Parmesan cheese
1	cup chopped pecans, toasted

Melt butter in a large skillet over medium heat; add chicken, and cook, stirring constantly, until browned. Remove chicken from skillet, reserving pan drippings in skillet; set chicken aside. Add mushrooms, scallions, red pepper, garlic, salt, and pepper to pan drippings in skillet, and sauté until vegetables are tender. Add chicken, and reduce heat and cook 15 minutes or until chicken is tender. Set aside, and keep warm. Place fettuccine in a large bowl. Add half-and-half, butter, parsley, salt, and pepper to fettuccine. Toss gently to combine. Add chicken mixture and Parmesan cheese to fettuccine, gently tossing to combine. Sprinkle with pecans and serve immediately.

Yield: 4-6 servings

CHICKEN MOROCCO

5	boneless chicken thighs
1½	cups onion, chopped
3	cloves garlic, minced
2	tablespoons olive oil
2	teaspoons paprika
¾	teaspoon salt
½	teaspoon turmeric
½	teaspoon ground coriander
½	teaspoon black pepper
½	teaspoon cumin
½	teaspoon ginger
1	(14-ounce) can diced tomatoes
1½	tablespoons lemon juice
1	large eggplant, peeled and cut in chunks
	Olive oil
¼	cup blanched, slivered almonds, toasted

The best: Bonny Doon Cigare Volant; the frugal alternative; Smoking Loon Syrah.

Preheat oven to 400°. Sauté onions and garlic in olive oil over medium heat, add paprika, salt, turmeric, coriander, pepper, cumin, and ginger. Stir 1 minute. Add tomatoes, lemon juice, and chicken. Bring to a boil. Lower heat, cover and simmer 20 minutes. Turn chicken pieces over and simmer another 20 minutes or until done. Place eggplant on a baking sheet greased with olive oil, roast for 20 minutes until brown, stirring occasionally. Mix eggplant into chicken stew; cook uncovered for 10 minutes until some of the liquid is reduced. Sprinkle with almonds.

Yield: 4-5 servings

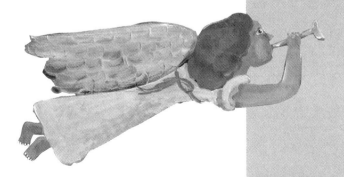

GREEN ENCHILADAS

3	chicken breasts
4	green bell peppers
1	(10-ounce) can green tomatillos or tomatillo salsa
4	sprigs parsley, finely chopped
½	small jar green chilies
1	cup heavy cream, divided
1	large egg
8	ounces cream cheese
1	onion, finely chopped
½	cup grated Parmesan cheese
2	cups grated Cheddar cheese
10-12	small corn tortillas
½	cup vegetable oil

Bruscus Reggiano Lambrusco pairs with the creamy, spicy enchiladas.

Place chicken breasts in large skillet and cover with water. Bring to a boil and simmer gently until they have turned white and are cooked through, about 20 minutes. Set aside to cool. Steam bell peppers until just soft, about 10 minutes, set aside to cool. Once cooled, slice peppers and, using a blender, combine drained tomatillos, parsley, green chilies, green peppers, ½ cup heavy cream, and egg into a thick purée. Shred cooled chicken breasts and, using a mixer, combine chicken pieces, cream cheese, chopped onion, and Parmesan cheese. Mix slowly until mixture is creamy and spreadable. Heat ½ cup vegetable oil in skillet and slowly heat each corn tortilla to soften. Spread each tortilla with about ⅓ cup chicken mixture, roll and place in baking dish. Cover enchiladas with pepper purée, remaining cream, and sprinkle with Cheddar cheese. Bake at 350° until bubbly.

Yield: 4 servings

SESAME-GINGER CORNISH HENS

½ cup soy sauce
¼ cup Dijon mustard
¼ cup packed dark brown sugar
2 tablespoons finely chopped and peeled fresh ginger
2 tablespoons oriental sesame oil
3 Cornish game hens cut in half lengthwise, backbones removed
Sesame seeds

Preheat oven to 425°. Whisk together soy sauce, mustard, sugar, ginger, and sesame oil in a medium bowl. Transfer half of marinade to a small saucepan; reserve. Pour remaining marinade into 15x10x2-inch glass baking dish. Add hens; turn to coat. Marinate 3 minutes at room temperature or up to four hours in the refrigerator, turning occasionally. Arrange hens, skin side up, on large rimmed baking sheet. Sprinkle with sesame seeds. Roast until cooked through and brown, about 40 minutes. Transfer to a platter and keep warm. Pour pan juices into saucepan with reserved marinade. Bring to boil, stirring often. Simmer until sauce coats spoon, about 5 minutes; pour into bowl. Serve hens with sauce.

Yield: 6 servings

Domaines Schlumberger Gewürztraminer loves Asian flavors

GLAZED CORNISH HENS

WILD RICE STUFFING

1	cup long-grain and wild rice mix, cooked in chicken stock
4	tablespoons butter, divided
1	medium onion, chopped
½	pound mushrooms, sliced
¼	cup celery, chopped
½	cup pecans
2	tablespoons chopped fresh parsley
¼	teaspoon thyme
¼	teaspoon marjoram
	Salt and black pepper, to taste

HENS

4	Cornish game hens
2	tablespoons butter, softened

CURRANT SAUCE

1	tablespoon butter
½	cup currant jelly
2	tablespoons fresh lemon juice
¼	cup cider vinegar, mixed with 1 tablespoon cornstarch to make a paste
3	whole cloves

Preheat oven to 350°. Prepare wild rice stuffing by combining the cooked rice with 2 tablespoons of butter and toss with a fork to fluff. Sauté onion, mushrooms, and celery in remaining butter. Add to rice and toss with pecans, parsley, thyme, marjoram, salt, and pepper. Stuff game hens. Rub skin with softened butter. Bake for ½ hour, then baste every 15 minutes with currant sauce until hens have baked for 1 ½ hours. Prepare currant sauce while hens cook. Melt butter, add jelly and lemon juice. After jelly has melted, add vinegar mixture, and cloves. Cook until thickened.

Yield: 4 servings

Meinklang Blanc de Noir is an elegant choice.

Marcel has good taste in wine and always knows what to order and it always tastes delicious, but to put a wine and food together is the other side of the story.

PORK CHOPS WITH SHALLOTS AND CIDER

- 8   (1-inch thick) rib pork chops (4 pounds total)
- 1   teaspoon fine sea salt
- 1¼ teaspoons black pepper
- 2½ tablespoons unsalted butter, divided
- 1   pound large shallots (8), bulbs separated if necessary and each bulb halved lengthwise
- 1   cup hard cider

Preheat oven to 450°. Pat pork chops dry and sprinkle both sides with sea salt and pepper. Heat 1½ tablespoons butter in a 12-inch heavy skillet over moderately high heat until foam subsides, then brown chops in 3 batches, turning once, 6 minutes per batch, and transfer with tongs to a large 1-inch deep baking pan. Add shallots and remaining tablespoon of butter to skillet and cook over moderate heat, turning occasionally, until golden brown and tender, 6-8 minutes. Add cider and boil, stirring and scraping up brown bits until reduced to about ¾ cup, about 3 minutes. Spoon shallots and sauce around chops and roast in lower third of oven 7-9 minutes. Let chops stand, loosely covered with foil, 5 minutes. Serve chops with shallots and sauce.

Cook's Note: Hard cider is available in small bottles from wine shops and some grocery stores.

A Riesling such as the George Albrecht Schneider Niersteiner Paterberg Riesling Kabinett pairs well with the cider in this recipe.

Yield: 8 servings

CHERRY BALSAMIC PORK CHOPS

SAUCE

- 3 tablespoons balsamic vinegar
- 3 tablespoons granulated sugar
- ¾ cup dry red wine
- ¼ cup minced shallots
- 1 (3-inch) cinnamon stick
- 1 cup chicken stock or prepared low-sodium broth
- ¾ cup (about 4 ounces) dried sour cherries
- 1 tablespoon cornstarch stirred together with 1 tablespoon cold water
- 2 teaspoons fresh lime juice, or to taste
- ¼ teaspoon salt
- ⅛ teaspoon freshly ground black pepper

CHOPS

- 8 (¾-inch) thick boneless pork loin chops (2 pounds total)
- 1 teaspoon salt
- ½ teaspoon freshly ground black pepper
- 2 tablespoons vegetable oil, divided

Combine vinegar and sugar in a 2-quart heavy saucepan, bring to a boil over moderate heat stirring, until a boil is reached, continue stirring until reduced to a glaze, about 4 minutes (be careful not to burn glaze). Add wine, shallots, and cinnamon stick, bring to a boil, and cook until reduced to about ¼ cup, about 10 minutes. Add stock and cherries; bring to a simmer, and simmer, uncovered, until cherries plump, about 5 minutes. Stir cornstarch mixture, add to sauce, and simmer, uncovered, whisking occasionally, for 2 minutes. Discard cinnamon stick, stir in lime juice, salt, and pepper. Remove from heat and keep sauce warm, covered. (This step may be done early in the day, and gently re-heated.) Pat chops dry and sprinkle with salt and pepper. Heat 1 tablespoon vegetable oil in a 12-inch heavy skillet over high heat until just smoking. Cook half the chops, turning once, until just cooked through, 6-8 minutes total. Transfer chops to a platter and loosely

Volnays are known for their cherry character. The best: J.M. Boillot; the frugal alternative: Smoking Loon Pinot Noir

cover with foil to keep warm. Cook remaining chops in remaining 1 tablespoon oil in same manner. Serve chops with sauce spooned over.

Cook's Note: *Tart and sweet, beautiful color, and a hint of cinnamon make this a yummy sauce for pork chops. It would also go well over pork tenderloin.*

Yield: 8 servings

HOISIN AND HONEY GLAZED PORK CHOPS

¼	cup Asian oyster sauce
2	tablespoons Dijon mustard
2	tablespoons hoisin sauce
1	teaspoon finely grated peeled fresh ginger
2	tablespoons honey
1	tablespoon soy sauce
1	bunch scallions, trimmed and cut diagonally into 2-inch pieces
4	pork chops (2 pounds total), 1-inch thick
	Steamed rice

Preheat oven to 400°. Whisk together oyster sauce, mustard, hoisin sauce, ginger, honey, and soy sauce in a large bowl. Add scallions and pork, turning pork to coat generously with sauce. Arrange pork in one layer in a 15x10-inch shallow baking pan (1-inch deep). Spoon remaining sauce with scallions over pork and roast until just cooked through, 15-20 minutes. Turn on broiler and broil pork 5-6 inches from heat until top is slightly caramelized, 2-5 minutes. Let stand, uncovered, 5 minutes. Serve pork topped with any pan juices; accompany with steamed rice.

Yield: 4 servings

The perfect pairing is Forrester's Petit Chenin.

My mother made plain food, which, when you're growing up and you're hungry all the time, was absolutely delicious. She made French fries from scratch, apple pie, which was delicious, delicious spaghetti and delicious French toast—all good things. I didn't like the soups or stews she made because they didn't fill me up. I loved pork chops and parsley potatoes and fresh green beans.

ROASTED PORK TENDERLOIN WITH HONEY-MUSTARD SAUCE

3	pounds pork tenderloin, whole
1½	teaspoons salt
¾	teaspoon freshly ground black pepper
2	tablespoons vegetable oil
2	cloves garlic, minced
2	tablespoons shallots, minced
1	tablespoon tomato paste
2	tablespoons whole-grain mustard
2	tablespoons honey
2½	tablespoons red wine vinegar
1½	teaspoons thyme, chopped
½	teaspoon salt
1	teaspoon black peppercorns, crushed
1⅓	cups vegetable or chicken broth

Preheat oven to 425°. Place a rack in a roasting pan, spray with nonstick spray, and place in oven. Remove any excess fat or silverskin from the tenderloin. Season the tenderloin with salt and pepper. Heat the vegetable oil in a large sauté pan over medium-high heat. Sear the tenderloin until it is golden brown on all sides, approximately 5 minutes. Remove the tenderloin and place it on the rack in the roasting pan. Roast 15-20 minutes. While the tenderloin is roasting, return the sauté pan to medium heat. Add the garlic and shallots; cook until fragrant, about 1 minute. Add the tomato paste and cook until slightly browned. Add the mustard, honey, vinegar, thyme, salt, peppercorns, and chicken broth. Bring to a boil, and simmer until the mixture reduces to a sauce consistency, about 10 minutes. Keep warm. Remove the tenderloins from the oven and let stand 5-10 minutes before slicing. Carefully skim and discard the fat from the pan juices. Pour the degreased pan juices into the sauce. Bring the sauce to a boil, reduce the heat, and simmer until it is slightly reduced. Slice the roast and serve with warm honey-mustard sauce.

Yield: 8 servings

The best: Jaboulet Aine, Paul Cornas Syrah, a great Northern Rhône, or Alain Voge; the frugal alternative: Domaine Pesquier Côtes du Rhône

I loved plain cooking. When I was about 12, I remember pretending that I was a horse named Scarlet Devil. I would gallop all around town. My mother would whistle for the horse and I would gallop home as fast as I could. When I'd get home, if we were having pork chops and parsley potatoes, I'd be so happy. If we were having stew, it was horrible!

CARIBBEAN PORK TENDERLOIN

PORK
2	teaspoons salt
½	teaspoon freshly ground black pepper
1	teaspoon ground cumin
1	teaspoon chili powder
1	teaspoon ground cinnamon
2	pork tenderloins, 2¼-2½ pounds total, trimmed
2	tablespoons olive oil

GLAZE
1	cup packed dark brown sugar
2	tablespoons finely chopped garlic
1	tablespoon hot pepper sauce

Château Le Devoy Martin Lirac Laurent Miquel Chardonnay Viognier is a perfect pairing with this sweet-spicy dish.

Preheat oven to 350°. Stir together salt, pepper, cumin, chili powder, and cinnamon in a small bowl. Coat pork with spice rub. Heat oil in an ovenproof 12-inch heavy skillet over moderately high heat until just beginning to smoke. Brown pork, turning occasionally, about 4 minutes total. Remove from heat; leave pork in skillet. Stir together brown sugar, garlic, and pepper sauce in a small bowl. Pat the mixture onto tops of tenderloins. Roast about 20 minutes. Let pork stand in skillet, loosely covered with foil, for 10 minutes. Cut pork at a 45° angle into ½-inch thick slices, and arrange on platter. Pour any juices from skillet over pork.

Yield: 6 servings

GRILLED PORK TENDERLOIN CUBAN-STYLE

4 cloves garlic, minced
1½ teaspoons salt, divided
5 tablespoons fresh orange juice
3 tablespoons olive oil, divided
1 teaspoon dried oregano, crumbled, divided
2 pork tenderloins, 1½ pounds total, trimmed
½ teaspoon freshly ground black pepper, divided

The best: Domaine Weinbach Muscat, an intriguing Alsace wine, is not sweet like other Muscat; the frugal alternative: Weingut Hillinger Welschriesling, not a Riesling at all, is quite good.

Prepare a charcoal or gas grill. Using a mortar and pestle, mash garlic to a paste with ½ teaspoon salt or mince and mash with a large heavy knife. Whisk garlic paste together with orange juice, 2 tablespoons oil, and ½ teaspoon oregano in a small bowl. Set sauce aside. Pat pork dry. Rub each tenderloin with 1½ teaspoons oil, ½ teaspoon salt, ¼ teaspoon oregano, and ¼ teaspoon pepper. Lightly oil grill rack. Grill pork, covered, turning once, until thermometer inserted diagonally into center of each tenderloin registers 150°, 10-14 minutes. Transfer pork to a cutting board and let stand, loosely covered with foil, for 10 minutes. Slice pork and serve drizzled with the citrus sauce.

Yield: 4 servings

JAMAICAN PORK KEBABS

- 5 scallions, chopped
- ½ cup cilantro, leaves and stems, chopped
- 1 inch piece of ginger, peeled, chopped
- 3 cloves garlic, chopped
- 1½ teaspoons ground allspice
- 2 teaspoons dried thyme
- 2 teaspoons Creole mustard
- ½ teaspoon cinnamon
- 1 jalapeño, seeded, chopped
- 1 teaspoon salt, or to taste
  Freshly ground black pepper, to taste
- 2 tablespoons Worcestershire sauce
- 2 tablespoons lime juice
- 3 tablespoons canola oil
- 3 pounds boneless pork loin, cut into 12 equal pieces
- 2 red peppers, cut into 1-inch pieces
- 2 yellow peppers, cut into 1-inch pieces
- 2 red onions, cut into 1-inch pieces

Serve with a light red that can be served cool or cold, such as Bruscus Reggiano Lambrusco

Combine scallions, cilantro, ginger, garlic, allspice, thyme, mustard, cinnamon, jalapeño, salt, and pepper in food processor. Pulse machine on and off until the mixture is coarsely chopped. Drizzle in Worcestershire sauce, lime juice, and then oil with the machine running, until a paste forms. Transfer mixture to a zip-lock bag, with the pork. Press out air, seal, turn, and gently squeeze bag several times until the pork is evenly coated. Let pork marinate at room temperature for at least 10 minutes before pre-heating the grill. Thread pork, peppers, and onions on skewers and grill over medium-high heat, turning as necessary, until pork is fully cooked and vegetables are hot and tender, about 15 minutes total. Serve at once.

Yield: 8 servings

MARINATED PORK TENDERLOIN

MEAT

2   pork tenderloins

MARINADE

½   cup peanut oil
⅓   cup soy sauce
¼   cup red wine vinegar
3   tablespoons lemon juice
2   tablespoons Worcestershire sauce
1-2 tablespoons minced, prepared garlic
1   tablespoon dry mustard
1½ teaspoons black pepper

Mix marinade ingredients thoroughly. Place pork in baking dish and pour marinade over pork. Marinate at least 8 hours, or overnight. Cook on grill until pink inside.

Yield: 6 servings

PORK TENDERLOIN RUB

1   tablespoon paprika
½   teaspoon chili powder
½   teaspoon freshly ground black pepper
1   teaspoon celery salt
1   teaspoon lemon pepper seasoning
¼   teaspoon garlic powder
¼   teaspoon onion powder
¼   teaspoon ground cayenne pepper
½   teaspoon salt
1   tablespoon dark brown sugar
    Olive oil

Mix everything together in a bowl and store in a screw-top jar. All will not be needed for just one piece of meat or ribs, so store in the refrigerator and use again. Rub the pork tenderloins or ribs with olive oil and then rub all over with the spice mixture. Grill or bake until cooked.

Yield: approximately ¼-cup rub

PINEAPPLE CHUTNEY

3	(15-ounce) cans of pineapple tidbits, drained
3	cups chopped onions
3	cups sugar (can substitute sugar substitute in part or whole)
2	cups golden raisins
1	cup cider vinegar
1	yellow bell pepper, chopped
1	orange bell pepper, chopped
1	tablespoon lemon zest
3-4	tablespoons lemon juice
2	teaspoons salt
1	tablespoon dried mustard
2	teaspoons celery seeds
½	teaspoon ground turmeric or saffron

Pineapple and wine don't mix.

In a large non-reactive pan, combine all ingredients. Stirring constantly, bring mixture to a boil over medium heat. Reduce heat to medium low. Continue to stir occasionally and simmer, uncovered, 50-60 minutes. Mixture will be thick. Spoon into heat resistant jars and store in the refrigerator.

Cook's Note: *Excellent with ham or pork tenderloin.*

Yield: 8 cups

SHERRY VINEGAR GLAZE FOR PORK TENDERLOIN

½-¾	teaspoon Sherry or balsamic vinegar Bitters
2-3	tablespoons maple syrup
1	teaspoon Dijon mustard
1	tablespoon fresh lemon juice

Mix together the vinegar, a generous dash of bitters, the syrup, mustard, and lemon juice.

Cook's Note: *For a variation, mix in 1 teaspoon minced garlic.*

Yield: ¼ cup

178

SPICE-CRUSTED HAM WITH MAPLE MUSTARD SAUCE

1	(8-10-pound) fully cooked shank-end ham
4	cloves garlic
1½	teaspoons fine sea salt
1	tablespoon whole coriander seeds
1	tablespoon mixed peppercorns (containing black, pink, white, and green peppercorns, but not allspice)
1	tablespoon all-purpose flour
3	tablespoons unsalted butter, softened
½	cup Dijon mustard
¼	cup pure maple syrup

Preheat oven to 350°. Remove any thick skin from ham and all but about ⅛-inch layer of fat. Mince and mash garlic with sea salt to a paste. Coarsely grind coriander and peppercorns in coffee/spice grinder and stir together with flour, butter, and garlic paste in a bowl. Spread spice paste all over ham, and then put ham, cut side down, in a greased large roasting pan. Bake about 1¼ hours. Make the mustard sauce by combining the mustard and the maple syrup; mixing until combined well. Set aside. Transfer ham to platter and let stand 15 minutes before slicing. Serve with mustard sauce.

Yield: 8 servings

Saint André de Figuière Côtes de Provence pairs well with the ham and mustard sauce.

SPICY ASIAN FLANK STEAK AND GREEN BEANS

3	tablespoons soy sauce
5	tablespoons rice wine vinegar
½	teaspoon toasted sesame oil
1	teaspoon Asian garlic-chili sauce
1	teaspoon olive or vegetable oil
1½	pounds skirt or flank steak
	Coarse salt and freshly ground black pepper
½	pound green beans, washed and trimmed
½	cup chopped scallions
	Cooked brown or white rice

Combine the soy, vinegar, sesame oil, and chile sauce in a small bowl and set aside. Heat a large skillet over high heat. Add vegetable oil, swirling to coat the pan. Sprinkle the steaks on all sides with salt and pepper and add to hot pan. Cook steaks, without moving, about 3-4 minutes, turn over and cook 3-4 more minutes on the other side. Transfer meat to a plate and cover with foil to keep warm. Pour off any excess fat from the pan. Add the green beans to the pan with ⅓ cup of water. Reduce the heat to medium, cover, and cook until the beans are crisp-tender, 4-5 minutes, adding more water if the pan gets too dry. Thinly slice the beef against the grain. Pour the soy mixture into the pan with the beans and scallions, and add the sliced beef along with any accumulated juices. Cook, uncovered, until just heated through, 1-2 minutes. Toss to combine and serve immediately with rice.

Yield: 4 servings

Lambrusco is the perfect pairing with the Asian spices.

In the last 8 years, I've been to California a lot and have had my best most important food experiences. My taste buds have developed more, and I've learned to blend wines with foods. Before, I knew if something tasted good, but I didn't learn to combine things until I started going out to California.

GRILLED FLANK STEAK WITH BALSAMIC MUSHROOMS

3½ pounds flank steak
Salt and black pepper to taste
4 large shallots
⅓ cup balsamic vinegar
¼ cup granulated sugar
¼ cup soy sauce

BALSAMIC MUSHROOMS

1½ pounds Portabella mushrooms
1½ pounds cremini mushrooms
3 large shallots
½ cup unsalted butter
6 scallions, green parts only
½ cup balsamic vinegar
5 tablespoons soy sauce
¼ cup granulated sugar
Salt and black pepper to taste

A Lodali Barbaresco compliments the beef, the mushrooms, and the fragrant sauce.

Pat steak dry and cut crosswise at a 45° angle into 4 equal pieces. Season steaks with salt and pepper and transfer to a large sealable heavy-duty plastic bag. Chop shallots and in a bowl stir together with vinegar, sugar, and soy sauce. Pour marinade into bag. Marinate steaks, covered and chilled, turning plastic bag over at least once, at least 2 hours, and up to 2 days. Prepare mushrooms. Halve Portabella mushrooms and cut into ¼-inch thick slices. Cut cremini mushrooms into ¼-inch slices. Chop shallots and in a 12-inch skillet cook half of the shallots in half of butter over moderate heat stirring, 1 minute. Add Portabellas and cook, stirring until mushroom liquid has evaporated, about 15 minutes. Transfer Portabellas to a bowl and cover. Cook remaining shallots in remaining butter, 1 minute. Add cremini and cook stirring until mushroom liquid has evaporated, about 10 minutes. Add cremini to Portabellas and cover. Mushrooms may be prepared up to this point 1 day ahead and chilled, covered. Diagonally, cut scallions into thin slices. In a bowl, whisk vinegar, soy sauce, and sugar. Heat mushrooms over moderate heat and add vinegar mixture. Boil 3 minutes, or until liquid is reduced slightly, and stir in scallions. Season with salt and pepper to taste. Prepare grill. Remove steaks from bag and discard marinade. Grill steaks on a lightly oiled rack set 5-6 inches over glowing coals 7-9 minutes on each side for medium-rare. Transfer steaks to a cutting board and let stand 10 minutes. Cut steak at a 45° angle across grain into thin slices. Serve steak with mushrooms on a large earthenware platter.

Yield: 8 servings

The best: Château Ducru-Beaucaillou; the frugal alternative: Domaine de Gournier Merlot.

HERBED FLANK STEAK

1	cup red wine
⅔	cup olive oil
½	teaspoon Worcestershire sauce
2	tablespoons chopped fresh parsley
2	bay leaves
2	scallions, chopped
3	cloves garlic, minced
1	teaspoon dried oregano
1	teaspoon salt
½	teaspoon black pepper
2	pounds flank steak
	Rosemary sprigs
2	tablespoons lemon juice

Combine red wine, olive oil, Worcestershire, parsley, bay leaves, scallions, garlic, oregano, salt, and pepper. Reserve ⅓ cup red wine mixture. Place flank steak in a large heavy-duty zip-lock plastic bag. Pour red wine mixture over steak. Cover or seal, and chill 2-4 hours, turning occasionally. Remove steak from marinade. Grill, covered with grill lid, over medium high heat for 8-10 minutes on each side or until desired doneness, brushing with reserved marinade combined with the rosemary sprigs. Cut steak diagonally across the grain into thin strips. Squeeze lemon juice over steak before serving.

Cook's Note: *This preparation also works well with lamb. Serve with simple olive oil roasted new potatoes.*

Yield: 6-8 servings

BEEF TENDERLOIN WITH MUSHROOMS AND ESPAGNOLE SAUCE

The best: Marimar Torres Don Miguel Vineyard Pinot Noir; the frugal alternative: Protocolo.

BEEF
- 2 (2½-pound) pieces trimmed center-cut beef tenderloin roast
- 1 tablespoon Kosher salt
- 2 teaspoons black pepper
- 3 tablespoons vegetable oil
- 3 tablespoons unsalted butter
- ½ pound small fresh cremini mushrooms, cut into ½-inch wedges

ESPAGNOLE SAUCE
- 1 small carrot, coarsely chopped
- 1 medium onion, coarsely chopped
- ¼ cup unsalted butter
- ¼ cup all-purpose flour
- 4 cups hot beef stock
- ¼ cup prepared tomato purée
- 2 large cloves garlic, coarsely chopped
- 1 stalk celery, coarsely chopped
- ½ teaspoon whole black peppercorns
- 1 bay leaf
- ½ cup medium-dry Sherry

Preheat oven to 425°. Remove any strings from beef if tied, then pat beef dry and sprinkle with salt and pepper. Heat oil in a deep 12-inch heavy skillet over high heat until just smoking, then sear beef 1 piece at a time, turning with tongs, until well browned, about 5 minutes each. (If beef tenderloin pieces are too long to fit into skillet, halve each crosswise, and then brown 2 pieces at a time.) Transfer beef to an 18x12-inch flameproof roasting pan, reserving skillet. Roast beef in oven 20-25 minutes. Transfer beef to a cutting board, reserving roasting pan, and let stand, loosely covered with foil, 25 minutes. While beef roasts, heat butter in skillet over moderately high heat until foam subsides, then reduce heat to moderate and cook mushrooms, stirring, until all liquid is evaporated and mushrooms are pale golden, 8-10 minutes.

Remove from heat. Set aside. Make espagnole sauce. Cook carrot and onion in butter in a 3-quart heavy saucepan over moderate heat, stirring occasionally, until golden, 7-8 minutes. Add flour and cook roux over moderately low heat, stirring constantly, until medium brown, 6-10 minutes. Add hot stock in a fast stream, whisking constantly to prevent lumps, add tomato purée, garlic, celery, peppercorns, and bay leaf and bring to a boil, stirring. Reduce heat and simmer, uncovered, stirring occasionally, until reduced to about 3 cups, about 45 minutes. Pour sauce through a fine-mesh sieve into a bowl, discarding solids. Set aside. While beef stands, straddle roasting pan across 2 burners, add Sherry and deglaze pan by boiling over high heat, stirring and scraping up brown bits, 1 minute. Add Sherry mixture and espagnole sauce to mushrooms and cook over moderate heat, stirring, until warm. Cover skillet and remove from heat. Cut meat crosswise into 10 or 20 slices. Pour any juices on cutting board into sauce and heat over moderate heat, stirring, until hot. Serve sauce with beef.

Cook's Note: *Wonderful! Sauce can be made the day before.*

Yield: 10 servings

When I understood what wine could do for food, that was a revelation to me. Wine was always just what you had...red wine with red meat, you know...and I always liked good wine, but the combination of learning to blend wine with food was just wonderful.

BEEF SHORT RIBS IN CHIPOTLE-GREEN CHILI SAUCE

1	teaspoon salt
1	teaspoon fresh ground black pepper
½	teaspoon ground cumin
1	teaspoon chili powder
½	teaspoon ground coriander
8	meaty short ribs of beef
2	tablespoons olive oil
1½	cups chopped onion
6	cloves garlic, minced
1	(14-ounce) can low sodium chicken broth
1	cup drained canned diced tomatoes
¼	cup fresh lime juice
1½	tablespoons chopped prepared chipotle chilies
	Salt and black pepper to taste
3	large fresh Anaheim chilies, stemmed, seeded, cut into ¼-inch-thick rings
	Chopped fresh cilantro to taste
	Lime wedges for garnish
	Soft tortilla shells

Mix salt, pepper, cumin, chili powder, and coriander in a bowl; sprinkle over short ribs. Transfer to plate, cover and chill 1 hour or up to 1 day. Preheat oven to 350°. Heat oil in large ovenproof pot over medium-high heat. Add half of ribs and brown on all sides, about 9 minutes; transfer to plate. Repeat with remaining ribs. Reduce heat to medium. Add onion and garlic to same pot; cover and cook until onion is soft, stirring occasionally, about 5 minutes. Add broth and bring to boil, scraping up browned bits. Add tomatoes, lime juice, and chipotle chilies. Return ribs to pot, meaty side down, in single layer. Bring to boil; cover and cook in oven until ribs are just tender, about 1½ hours. Remove pot from oven. Tilt pot; spoon off fat. Place pot over medium heat and simmer uncovered until sauce coats spoon and ribs are very tender, about 25 minutes. Season sauce with salt and pepper. (Recipe to this point may be made 1 day ahead. Cool 30 minutes, refrigerate uncovered until cold, then cover and

Lambrusco is the perfect wine to offset the spiciness of this dish.

keep refrigerated.) Bring ribs to simmer over medium heat; add chili rings. Simmer until chilies soften, about 10 minutes. Transfer ribs and sauce to large bowl. Sprinkle with cilantro; garnish with lime wedges. Serve with warmed, soft tortilla shells.

Cook's Note: *Chipotle chilies, canned in a spicy tomato sauce, sometimes called adobo, are available at Latin American markets, specialty foods stores, and some supermarkets.*

Yield: 6 servings

The best: Scala Dei Cartoixa Reserva; the frugal alternative: Finca Luzon.

BEEF FILLET MADAGASCAR

4	beef fillets (6-8 ounces each)
2	tablespoons olive oil
½	onion, diced
4	cloves garlic, minced
¼	cup brandy or Cognac
1	tablespoon green peppercorns
1	tablespoon demi-glaze (concentrated)
¼	cup heavy cream

Heat olive oil in a large skillet then add steaks. Cook the steaks to desired doneness, season to taste and set aside to rest. In the same pan sauté the onion and garlic then deglaze the pan with the brandy. Add green peppercorns, demi-glaze, and cream and reduce sauce to desired thickness Serve sauce over fillets.

Cook's Note: *Demi-glaze may be purchased at a specialty food store.*

Yield: 6 servings

GRILLED DIJON-PEPPER RIB ROAST WITH SOUR CREAM HORSERADISH SAUCE

The best: Château Latour-à-Pomerol; the frugal alternative: Step Road Blackwing Merlot.

BEEF

- 1½ tablespoons black peppercorns
- 1 boneless beef rib roast (2½ - 3 pounds), well trimmed
- ¼ cup Dijon mustard
- 2 cloves garlic, minced

SOUR CREAM HORSERADISH SAUCE

- ¾ cup sour cream
- 2 tablespoons prepared horseradish
- 1 tablespoon balsamic vinegar
- ½ teaspoon granulated sugar

Prepare grill for indirect cooking. Place peppercorns in small plastic food storage bag. Squeeze out excess air; close bag securely. Pound peppercorns until cracked, using flat side of meat mallet or rolling pin. Set aside. Pat roast dry with paper towels. Combine mustard and garlic in small bowl; spread over top and sides of roast. Sprinkle peppercorns over mustard mixture. Place roast, pepper-side up, on grill cook, covered, over medium heat 1 hour-1 hour 10 minutes for medium. Meanwhile, prepare Sour Cream Sauce, if using, by combining the sour cream, horseradish, vinegar, and sugar, mixing well. Cover and refrigerate until ready to use. Transfer roast to cutting board; cover with foil. Let stand 10-15 minutes before carving. Serve with Sour Cream Horseradish Sauce, if desired.

Cook's Note: *A wonderful dinner party recipe.*

Yield: 6-8 servings

GRILLED LAMB CHOPS WITH BALSAMIC GRAPE TOMATOES

2	tablespoons honey
2	tablespoons red-wine vinegar
2	cloves garlic, finely chopped
½	teaspoon salt
¼	teaspoon black pepper
8	rib lamb chops, boned Frenched and all fat trimmed
1½	pounds grape tomatoes
1½	tablespoons balsamic vinegar

Stir together honey, vinegar, garlic, salt, and pepper and transfer to a zip-lock bag. Add lamb, seal bag, pressing out excess air and turning to distribute marinade. Marinate lamb, chilled, turning occasionally, 1 hour. Bring lamb to room temperature. Prepare grill. Remove lamb from marinade, reserving marinade. Grill lamb, about 4 minutes for medium-rare. Transfer to a platter and keep warm, covered. Cook tomatoes in a roasting pan, on the grill covered with grill lid, carefully turning, until softened and just beginning to split, about 8 minutes. Drizzle balsamic vinegar over tomatoes, turning to coat, cooking, uncovered, until vinegar is reduced by about half, about 2 minutes. Remove from grill. Bring reserved marinade with any lamb juices accumulated on platter to a boil in a small heavy saucepan, covered. Drizzle lamb with marinade and serve with tomatoes.

Cook's Note: Lamb and tomatoes may also be grilled in batches in a lightly oiled well-seasoned ridged grill pan over moderately high heat (tomatoes will take less time to soften, about 3 minutes).

Yield: 4 servings

The best: Kay Brothers Amery Vineyards Block 6 Shiraz; the frugal alternative: Milton Park Shiraz.

188

GRILLED LEG OF LAMB WITH LEMON, HERBS, AND GARLIC

6	cloves garlic, finely chopped
3	tablespoons chopped fresh thyme leaves
2	tablespoons chopped fresh rosemary leaves
2	tablespoons chopped fresh parsley leaves
½	teaspoon freshly ground black pepper
I	tablespoon coarse salt
3	tablespoons olive oil
7-8	pound leg of lamb, trimmed of all fat, boned, and butterflied
I	lemon

The best:
Tittarelli Malbec;
the frugal alternative:
Musaragno Malbec.

To make herb rub, combine garlic, thyme, rosemary, parsley, pepper, salt, and oil in a small bowl. Put lamb in a large dish and with tip of a sharp small knife held at a 45-degree angle cut ½-inch-deep slits all over lamb, rubbing herb mixture into slits and all over lamb. Marinate lamb at room temperature I hour. Prepare grill. Lightly pat lamb dry. Grill lamb about 10 minutes on each side. (Alternatively, roast lamb in a roasting pan in middle of a 425° oven, about 25 minutes.) Transfer lamb to a cutting board. Halve and seed lemon. Squeeze juice over lamb and let stand, loosely covered with foil, 15 minutes. Cut lamb into slices and serve with any juices that have accumulated on cutting board.

Cook's Note: *Butterflied leg of lamb can sometimes get a little unwieldy. To secure loose flaps of meat, run 2 long metal skewers lengthwise and 2 skewers crosswise through the lamb, bunching the meat together. Securing the lamb this way will also help it cook more evenly.*

Yield: 8 servings

WINTER NIGHT LAMB SHANKS

6   small lamb shanks (or 3-4 large ones)
        Juice of ½ lemon
½   cup all-purpose flour
2   teaspoons salt
½   teaspoon black pepper
¼   cup olive oil
¾   cup onion, finely chopped
I   clove garlic, crushed or minced
I   (10½-ounce) can of beef consommé
I   cup water
I   bay leaf, crushed
½   cup carrots, finely chopped
½   cup celery, finely chopped

Preheat Oven to 375°. Rub lamb shanks with lemon juice; allow to stand for 10 minutes. Shake meat in paper bag with flour, salt, and pepper. Sauté meat in hot oil until well browned on all sides. Remove to a 4-quart casserole (with lid). Drain off all but 2 tablespoons fat. Sauté onion and garlic in lamb drippings until tender. Stir in any remaining seasoned flour and brown lightly. Add consommé, water, and bay leaf. Heat and stir until thickened. Pour over meat in the casserole. Scatter carrots and celery over meat. Cover and bake for two hours until the meat is very tender. Skim off any excess fat.

Cook's Note: *Serve over bulgur wheat pilaf for a hearty winter dinner.*

Yield: 4-6 servings

The best: Seghesio Old Vine Zinfandel; the frugal alternative: Kimball Zinfandel.

190

BALSAMIC-GINGERED LAMB SHANKS

The best:
Châteauneuf-du-
Pâpe, Domaine
de Pegau Cuveé
Reserveé, the frugal
alternative: André
Brunel Côtes
du Rhône.

¼ cup olive oil, divided
4 (12-ounce) domestic hind bone-in lamb shanks
1½ teaspoons Kosher salt, divided
1¼ teaspoons black pepper, divided
2 tablespoons chopped peeled fresh ginger
8 cloves garlic, thinly sliced
1 fennel bulb, trimmed, cored, and thinly sliced
1 Spanish onion, thinly sliced
½ teaspoon fennel seeds
¾ teaspoon crushed red pepper flakes
2 teaspoons ground cumin
⅔ cup dry red wine
1 cup balsamic vinegar
3 tomatoes, chopped or 1½ cups grape tomatoes
1 (15-ounce) can cooked white beans
3 fresh rosemary sprigs
10 cups water or canned low-sodium chicken broth

Preheat the oven to 350°. Place a large ovenproof skillet or a Dutch oven over medium-high heat and when hot, add 2 tablespoons of the oil. Sprinkle the lamb shanks with 1 teaspoon of the salt and 1 teaspoon of the pepper and add them to the pan. Cook until they are browned on both sides, about 4-5 minutes on each side. Set the shanks aside and discard the oil. Wipe the skillet clean and reheat it. Add the remaining 2 tablespoons oil. Add ginger and garlic, stirring well after each addition, and cook until the garlic is golden, about 3 minutes. Add the fennel, onion, fennel seeds, pepper flakes, cumin, the remaining ½ teaspoon salt, and ¼ teaspoon pepper, the wine, and vinegar, stirring well after each addition. Cook until the sauce has reduced somewhat, about 5 minutes. Add the tomatoes and white beans and return the shanks to the pan. Add the rosemary and liquid. Bring to a simmer, and then transfer the skillet to the oven. Bake, uncovered, until the meat is falling off the bone, about 3 hours.

Cook's Note: *While this calls for lots of ingredients, it is very simple and can be prepared earlier in the day and then reheated. Serve with mashed potatoes in colorful pasta bowls with a generous amount of sauce.*

Yield: 4 servings

The best: Spy
Valley Sauvignon
Blanc; the frugal
alternative: Zed
Sauvignon Blanc.

VEAL CHOPS WITH OLIVES AND CAPERS

	Sea salt or Kosher salt
4	veal chops, 1¼-inches thick
2	tablespoons butter, divided
1	clove garlic, minced
¾	cup dry white wine
¼	cup chopped tomato
1	tablespoon capers
3	tablespoons coarsely chopped Kalamata olives

Lightly coat the bottom of a skillet with the salt. Heat over medium high heat. Sear veal chops on one side for 1 minute, turn over and reduce the heat to medium low. Continue cooking, turning once, 5-6 minutes for medium rare. Remove from pan and keep warm. Melt 1 tablespoon of butter in the same skillet. Sauté garlic 1 minute. Add wine, turn heat to high and stir up browned bits in bottom of pan. Boil until wine is reduced in half. Stir in tomato, capers, and olives. Add remaining tablespoon of butter and stir until melted. Spoon sauce over chops and serve immediately.

Yield: 4 servings

VEAL CHOPS WITH SPINACH AND GRAPE TOMATOES

The best: Antinori
Orvietto; the frugal
alternative: Doña
Beatriz Rueda
Verdejo.

6	loin veal chops, each 1-1½-inches thick
	Salt and freshly ground black pepper
7	tablespoons olive oil, divided
2	cloves garlic, crushed, divided
1½	pounds fresh spinach, tough stems removed, well washed and drained, divided
1	cup freshly grated Pecorino-Romano cheese
1	pint grape tomatoes, stems removed and cut in half
4	fresh basil leaves, cut into thin strips

Prepare charcoal grill or heat two large grill pans over medium heat for 10 minutes. Pat veal chops dry with paper towels and season generously with salt and pepper. Rub 2 tablespoons of olive oil over chops. Grill chops, turning once, until both sides are well marked (or browned if using skillet) and just a slight trace of pink remains in the thickest part of the chop near the bone, about 15-18 minutes. Transfer chops to a broiler pan or sturdy baking pan and preheat broiler. Meanwhile, divide 3 tablespoons of olive oil between two large skillets. Add 1 clove garlic to each skillet and cook over medium heat until golden, about 3 minutes. Add half the spinach to each skillet and season very lightly with salt and pepper. Cook, stirring, until spinach is wilted and tender, 3-4 minutes. Season again with salt and pepper. Drain the liquid from skillets and remove garlic cloves, setting garlic aside. This may be done early in the day. Arrange spinach evenly over the veal chops, sprinkle with the grated cheese and set aside. In a large skillet, heat remaining 2 tablespoons olive oil over medium heat. Add the 2 garlic cloves and cook until lightly browned, about 2 minutes. Add the tomatoes, basil and season lightly with salt and pepper. Cook, tossing the tomatoes in the skillet, about 2 minutes. Remove the garlic. Remove from heat and cover to keep tomatoes warm. Broil the chops until the cheese is lightly browned and crisp, about 3 minutes. Transfer the veal chops to plates. Spoon tomatoes alongside the veal and serve hot.

Yield: 6 servings

PORTABELLA MUSHROOM PICATTA

4-6	medium Portabella mushrooms, stemmed and cleaned
2	cups all-purpose flour, divided
3	cups fresh breadcrumbs
½	bunch Italian parsley, chopped, divided
2	sprigs fresh thyme leaves, minced
1	sprig fresh rosemary leaves, minced
	Pinch salt and black pepper
1	teaspoon fennel seeds, toasted
3	large eggs, slightly beaten
1	tablespoon olive oil
½	tablespoon minced garlic
2	tablespoons freshly squeezed lemon juice
1	tablespoon capers with juice
4	tablespoons butter
2	scallions, thinly sliced at a diagonal (white and light green parts only)
1	small tomato, diced
	Salt and freshly ground black pepper

Sartori Amarone compliments the flavors of the mushrooms and spices.

Set aside 1 cup of the flour for dredging. Mix the remaining flour with the breadcrumbs, half of the parsley, thyme, rosemary, salt, pepper, and fennel seeds. Dredge the mushrooms with the plain flour. Dip into eggs, shaking off any excess, and coat well with crumb mixture. Heat olive oil in a medium sauté pan over medium-high heat. Add the mushrooms, being careful not to crowd the pan. Cook until well browned and tender, turning once, about 3-4 minutes on each side. Remove mushrooms from the pan to a warm serving plate. (Note: If the mushrooms have not browned evenly, place them under the broiler just until well browned. Due to the shape of some Portabella mushrooms, it can be difficult to brown them evenly in the pan.) In the same pan used for browning the mushrooms, add the garlic and cook, stirring constantly, for 1 minute. Add lemon juice, capers, butter, scallions, tomato, and a pinch each of salt and pepper. Shake the pan from side to side to incorporate the sauce. Pour warm sauce over mushrooms, garnish with the remaining parsley and serve immediately.

Cook's Note: *A good vegetarian main dish!*

Yield: 4-6 servings

GRILLED PORTABELLA MUSHROOM BURGERS WITH GARLIC AÏOLI

Deen VAT 1 Durif is the perfect accompaniment.

PORTABELLA BURGERS
8 large Portabella mushrooms, stems removed, cleaned
¼ cup olive oil
2 teaspoons Kosher salt
Canola oil for grilling
Tomatoes, lettuce, onions and buns for serving

GARLIC AÏOLI
2 egg yolks
1 teaspoon Dijon mustard
3 cloves garlic, finely minced
1 tablespoon lemon juice
½ cup extra virgin olive oil
½ cup canola oil
1¼ teaspoons Kosher salt

Brush mushrooms in olive oil and sprinkle with salt. Heat a rigid grill pan or outdoor grill on medium heat. Brush grill with canola oil. Grill mushrooms until soft, about 7 minutes per side, brushing with additional olive oil if they look dry. Make the sauce by whisking together eggs, mustard, garlic, and lemon juice beating until thick. Combine olive and canola oils and add to egg mixture in a steady stream. Do not add oil too quickly and be sure emulsion is stable (has absorbed oil) before adding more oil. Transfer to a small bowl. Season with salt and more lemon juice if needed. If mixture becomes too thick, add 2-3 tablespoons warm water to the aïoli, whisking constantly, to combine. Use sauce the day it is made.

Cook's Note: *May be served with tomatoes, lettuce, roasted red pepper or any of your favorite accompaniments with or without bun.*

Yield: 8 burgers and ½ cup aïoli

GRECIAN EGGPLANT WITH FETA AND TOMATOES

3	eggplants, about 1 pound each, trimmed and cut lengthwise into slices ¼-inch thick (about 16 slices total)
¾	cup olive oil, or as needed
	Coarse salt
8	ounces feta cheese, crumbled
½	cup pine nuts
¼	cup extra virgin olive oil, more for drizzling
2	tablespoons breadcrumbs
1	clove garlic, peeled and minced
	Finely grated zest of 1 lemon
1½	teaspoons dried mint
2	tablespoons chopped Italian parsley leaves
1	large egg, beaten
	Salt and freshly ground black pepper to taste
2½	cups drained canned crushed tomatoes
1	large ball fresh mozzarella, cut into ¼-inch slices

Santorini White is a good compliment to the tomatoes and cheese.

Heat oven to 375°. Place a heavy skillet over medium-high heat. Working in batches, brush eggplant slices on both sides with olive oil, salt lightly and cook, turning, until soft. Set aside and allow to cool. In a large bowl, combine feta, pine nuts, ¼-cup olive oil, breadcrumbs, garlic, lemon zest, mint, and parsley. Mix in egg, and season to taste with salt and pepper. Spread eggplant slices on a surface and divide stuffing evenly among them, placing 1-2 tablespoons at one end of each slice. Roll up slices tightly to secure filling, and place in a 9x13-inch baking dish. Pour crushed tomatoes on top of eggplant rolls. Arrange mozzarella slices in a line lengthwise down center of pan. Drizzle olive oil evenly over pan, and season to taste with salt and pepper. Bake until cheese has melted and eggplant is bubbling and fragrant, 25-30 minutes. Remove from heat and allow to stand 5-10 minutes. Serve hot.

Cook's Note: *A wonderful blend of flavors in a hearty vegetarian meal. Serve with a crusty whole wheat baguette and a citrus salad.*

Yield: 6 servings

POLENTA WITH PORCINI MUSHROOM SAUCE

The best: Penfold Yattarna Chardonnay; the frugal alternative: Milton Park Chardonnay.

POLENTA
- 4-5 cups water
- 2 tablespoons olive oil
- 1 teaspoon salt
- 1 cup yellow cornmeal
- 1¼ cups freshly grated Parmesan cheese
- ¼ cup butter

PORCINI SAUCE
- ½ ounce dried porcini mushrooms
- 1 cup warm water
- 2 tablespoons olive oil
- 1 cup chopped onion
- 2 cloves garlic, minced
- ½ cup dry Marsala
- ½ cup dry white wine
- 1 teaspoon minced fresh rosemary
- 1 cup chicken stock or prepared low-salt chicken broth
- 1 cup beef stock or prepared beef broth
- 1 tablespoon butter, room temperature
- 1 tablespoon all-purpose flour
- Salt and black pepper, to taste

Before starting polenta, re-hydrate dried porcinis by covering them with 1 cup warm water in small bowl. Let stand until mushrooms soften, about 30 minutes. To make polenta, combine water, oil, and salt in heavy large saucepan. Bring to boil. Gradually whisk in cornmeal. Reduce heat to low; cook until polenta is very thick, stirring occasionally, about 30 minutes. Stir in Parmesan cheese and butter. Polenta will stay warm for up to 20 minutes, covered, off the heat and will thicken as it cools. Make porcini sauce, by removing mushrooms from liquid, squeezing excess liquid from mushrooms back into bowl; reserve liquid. Place mushrooms in another small bowl. Heat oil in heavy large saucepan over medium-high heat. Add onion and garlic and sauté until onion is soft and golden, about 15 minutes. Add Marsala and white wine. Increase heat and boil until most liquid evaporates, about 7 minutes. Add rosemary, mushrooms, and both stocks. Strain mushroom liquid through a coffee filter into mixture. Pour in reserved mushroom liquid, leaving any sediment behind. Boil until liquid mixture is reduced to 2 cups, about 15 minutes. Mix butter and flour in small bowl to blend; whisk small bits into mushroom sauce until just thickened. Season with salt and pepper. Ladle polenta into shallow bowls and top with porcini sauce. Serve with additional grated cheese if desired.

Cook's Note: *Dried porcini mushrooms are available at most grocery and specialty food stores.*

Yield: 6 servings

Alessi Scacciapensieri Red Table Wine goes well with the tomatoes and balsamic vinegar.

PENNE WITH TOMATOES AND BALSAMIC VINEGAR

½	cup extra virgin olive oil
3-4	cloves garlic, thinly sliced
2	sprigs fresh rosemary, chopped
2	cups canned, peeled plum tomatoes, drained and reserved
	Freshly ground black pepper
	Salt to taste
1	pound penne pasta
2	teaspoons balsamic vinegar

Put olive oil in a skillet. Turn heat to medium. Add garlic and rosemary and cook until the oil sizzles. Add tomatoes, ½ cup of reserved liquid, pepper, and salt. Cook for 10 minutes. Turn heat off and let sit. Cook pasta in boiling water until al dente. Drain and add to the tomato mixture. Turn heat to low and cook for a minute to reheat sauce. Just before serving, drizzle the vinegar over all and mix in thoroughly.

Yield: 4-6 servings

PASTA WITH BELL PEPPERS, GOAT CHEESE, AND BASIL

2	cloves garlic, minced
2	tablespoons olive oil
½	cup finely chopped onion
1	large red bell pepper cut into julienne strips
1	large yellow bell pepper cut into julienne strips
⅓	cup dry white wine or dry vermouth
⅓	cup sliced pitted Kalamata or other brine-cured black olives
	Salt and black pepper to taste
½	cup finely-shredded fresh basil leaves
½	pound rotelle or fusilli pasta
3	ounces mild goat cheese, crumbled, divided

The best: Alan Scott Sauvignon Blanc; the frugal alternative: Graham Beck Sauvignon Blanc.

When traveling, I can't bring the food home. Seeing the display in the Paris markets…I'd never before seen food displayed like that. California also has some beautiful markets. There was a place in Palm Springs—just like a regular grocery store, like our Food Lion here, but it was California—and you'd go in and find the freshest vegetables, huge, everything bursting with flavor and beauty. It was just the local market, but was so amazing to me.

In a skillet cook garlic in oil over moderately-low heat, stirring, for 1 minute. Add onion, and cook the mixture, stirring, until the onion is softened. Add bell peppers, cook over moderate heat, stirring, for 5 minutes, or until the peppers are just tender. Add the wine and olives. Boil the wine until reduced by half, season the mixture with salt and pepper to taste, and stir in basil. In a kettle of boiling salted water cook the pasta until it is al dente, drain it well, reserving ⅓-cup of the cooking water. In a serving bowl whisk ⅔ of the goat cheese with the reserved cooking water until the cheese is melted and the mixture is smooth, add the pasta and the bell pepper mixture, tossing the mixture well. Sprinkle the pasta with the remaining goat cheese.

Yield: 2 servings

LINGUINE À LA CAPRESE

4	large tomatoes, cut into ½-inch dice
½	cup fresh basil, coarsely chopped
7	ounces fresh mozzarella cheese, cubed
2	teaspoons garlic, minced
	Freshly ground black pepper, to taste
⅓	cup extra virgin olive oil
12	ounces linguine
1	tablespoon olive oil
	Salt, to taste

In a pan combine tomatoes with basil, cheese, garlic, pepper, and oil. Heat on low heat. Cook pasta in boiling water, with the tablespoon of oil, for 10 minutes or until al dente. Drain and add to the tomato mixture. Toss well and season with salt to taste. Serve immediately.

Yield: 6 servings

Avignonesi Rosso di Toscana is the perfect accompaniment.

MACARONI AND THREE CHEESES

8	ounces elbow macaroni
2	cups cottage cheese
1	cup sour cream
1	large egg, beaten
¾	teaspoon salt
	Black pepper, to taste
8	ounces grated sharp Cheddar cheese
⅔	cup grated Parmesan cheese
	Paprika

Preheat oven to 350°. Cook macaroni according to package directions; drain and set aside. Combine cottage cheese, sour cream, egg, salt, and pepper. Add Cheddar cheese and mix well. Stir in macaroni. Place into a greased 7x11-inch dish. Sprinkle with Parmesan cheese and paprika. Bake 35-40 minutes.

Yield: 6-8 servings

Any wine from Champagne to Port will go well with this dish.

SPINACH PIE

I	pound fresh spinach, chopped
3-4	bunches scallions, chopped
	Salt, to taste
8	large eggs
I½	pounds feta cheese, crumbled
I½	cups butter, divided
I	(I-pound) box frozen filo pastry

Preheat oven to 350°. Wash spinach and combine with scallions. Lightly salt and drain. Squeeze out excess water. Beat eggs until well combined. In a medium bowl, mix crumbled cheese, spinach, onions, eggs, and ¾ cup melted butter. Grease a 10x13-inch pan with butter. Layer with 4 sheets filo dough, brushing each sheet with butter, and spread with ¼ of spinach mixture. Continue process 3 more times ending with 4 pastry sheets, brushing each with butter. Bake I hour. Cool and cut into squares.

Cook's Note: *Filo pastry is in the frozen foods section of the grocery store. Often, there are 2 packages of 20 sheets. A total of 20 sheets is needed for this recipe.*

Yield: 50 pieces

Desserts

Nancy Thomas

DESSERTS

CHOCOLATE AMARETTO TRUFFLES

2 cups milk chocolate morsels
¼ cup sour cream
2 tablespoons amaretto
2 cups chopped almonds

Melt chocolate morsels in top of a double boiler over hot water; stir until smooth. Remove from heat, and blend in sour cream. Add amaretto and mix well. Chill until firm. Drop by teaspoonfuls onto waxed paper. Shape into balls and roll in almonds. Chill 30 minutes.

Cook's Note: *Place in cellophane bags and tie with festive ribbons for a holiday gift.*

Yield: 2½ dozen pieces

FEATHERWEIGHT PEANUT BUTTER COOKIES

1 cup creamy or chunky peanut butter
1 cup granulated sugar
1 large egg, lightly beaten
1 teaspoon baking soda

Preheat oven to 350°. Lightly butter two large baking sheets. Beat together peanut butter and sugar in a medium bowl with an electric mixer at medium speed for 2 minutes or until well combined. Beat in egg and baking soda. Roll level teaspoons of dough into balls and place about 1-inch apart on buttered baking sheet. Flatten balls into 1½-inch rounds with tines of a fork, making a crosshatch pattern. Bake cookies in batches for about 10 minutes per batch until golden. Cool on baking sheets for 2 minutes, then transfer to racks to cool.

Cook's Note: *These cookies keep in an airtight container at room temperature for up to 5 days.*

Yield: 4½ dozen cookies

I had an unusual experience in Auberge du Soleil in California where they had oysters and I love oysters. So I ordered the starter, which was oysters, then I wanted my main course to be oysters. Then the waiter said, "Well what would you like for dessert?" I said, "Oysters!" I had a different wine with each one. The combinations were all just perfect.

CHOCOLATE CHUNK CELEBRATIONS

18 ounces semisweet baking chocolate, coarsely chopped
¼ pound unsalted butter, cut into ½-ounce pieces
1 cup all-purpose flour
1 teaspoon baking powder
¼ teaspoon salt
¾ cup plus 2 tablespoons granulated sugar
4 large eggs
1 tablespoon pure vanilla extract
1 cup pecans, toasted, and coarsely chopped
4 ounces semisweet baking chocolate, chopped into medium chunks

Preheat oven to 350°. Line each of 18 individual muffin tin cups with 2½-inch foil-laminated bake cups. Set aside. Melt 18 ounces chopped semisweet chocolate and the butter in the top half of a double boiler or in a medium glass bowl in a microwave oven, and stir until smooth. Set aside. In a sifter combine the flour, baking powder, and salt. Sift onto a large piece of parchment paper or wax paper and set aside. Place the sugar and eggs in the bowl of an electric mixer fitted with a paddle. Beat on medium speed for 2 minutes until light in color and slightly thickened. Scrape down the sides of the bowl and add the melted chocolate and butter mixture and mix on low speed for about five seconds to combine. Operate the mixer on low while gradually adding the sifted dry ingredients. Once all the dry ingredients have been incorporated, about 10 seconds, stop the mixer and scrape down the sides of the bowl. Add the vanilla extract and mix on low for 5 seconds. Remove the bowl from the mixer and use a rubber spatula to fold in the chopped pecans and chocolate chunks and finish mixing the batter until thoroughly combined. Portion 2 heaping tablespoons of the batter into each bake cup. Place the muffin tins in the preheated oven, and bake for about 18 minutes or until a toothpick inserted in the center of a chunk comes out almost clean, turning the muffin tins 180 degrees halfway through the baking time. Remove the cupcakes from the oven and cool at room

I really got interested in the whole food world because of my friendship with Marcel…which goes back 25 years. We like each other so much. When Marcel and Connie started buying my artwork we started talking and just out of friendship I did— I think it was for his first book— a big chef for him. From that point on, he asked me to do chefs for all his books. After that we became very good friends. Our friendship, never based on food, has been based on just us having a lot in common. He's one of those people I've been mortified

temperature in the tins for 10 minutes. Remove the cupcakes from the muffin tins, but not from the foil bake cups, and cool at room temperature for an additional 20 minutes.

Cook's Note: *The Chocolate Chunk Celebrations may be stored in a tightly sealed plastic container for 4-5 days.*

Marcel Desaulniers   Yield: 18 chunks

WHITE CHOCOLATE PECAN TRUFFLES

2	tablespoons heavy cream
3	ounces fine quality white chocolate, finely chopped
1	teaspoon unsalted butter, softened
2	teaspoons brandy
¾	cup pecans, coarsely chopped, toasted lightly, divided

In a small saucepan bring the cream to a boil, remove the pan from the heat, and add the chocolate, stirring until it is melted completely. Add the butter, stir the mixture until it is smooth, and stir in the brandy and ¼ cup of the pecans. Transfer the mixture to a bowl and chill it, covered, for 4 hours, or until it is firm. Form the mixture by teaspoons into balls and roll the balls in the remaining ½ cup pecans. Chill the truffles in a baking pan for 1 hour, or until they are firm.

Cook's Note: *The truffles keep in an airtight container, covered and chilled, for 1 week. These make a good gift at holiday time.*

Yield: 16 truffles

by at first, because he'd have something wonderful on the menu, I'd be having dinner with the two of them at the Trellis, he'd say, "What do you think of the taste of that?" And I'd say, "It's good!" I was just clueless!

204

PEANUT BUTTER-CHOCOLATE BARK TRIANGLES

10 ounces bittersweet (not unsweetened) chocolate, coarsely chopped

6 ounces good quality white chocolate, coarsely chopped

½ cup creamy peanut butter

1¾ cups chopped peanut brittle (about 8 ounces), divided

8 ounces good-quality milk chocolate, coarsely chopped

Turn large baking sheet upside down. Cover tightly with foil. Mark 12x9-inch rectangle on foil. Stir bittersweet chocolate in double boiler over barely simmering water (do not allow bottom of pan to touch water) until mixture is melted and candy thermometer registers 115°. Remove from heat. Spoon 2 tablespoons melted chocolate into small metal bowl; set aside. Pour remaining melted chocolate onto marked rectangle on foil. Using icing spatula, spread chocolate to fill rectangle. Refrigerate while making peanut butter filling. Stir chopped white chocolate and peanut butter continuously in heavy medium saucepan over medium-low heat until mixture is melted and smooth. Remove from heat. Cool mixture about 10 minutes to barely lukewarm. Pour over the chilled bittersweet chocolate. Working quickly, spread to coat chocolate completely. Sprinkle with ¾ cup chopped brittle. Chill about 20 minutes until very firm. Stir milk chocolate in double boiler over barely simmering water until chocolate is melted and candy thermometer registers 115°. Remove from over water. Pour chocolate over chilled brittle, spreading quickly to cover. Sprinkle with 1 cup brittle. Reheat reserved 2 tablespoons bittersweet chocolate over simmering water, stirring until warm. Dip spoon in chocolate and drizzle lines over brittle. Chill bark about 20 minutes until firm enough to cut. Lift foil with bark onto work surface. Cut crosswise into 5 approximately 2-inch wide strips. Cut each strip crosswise into 4 sections and diagonally into 2 triangles. (Can be made 2 weeks ahead. Chill in airtight container. Let stand at room temperature at least 30 minutes and up to 1 hour before serving.)

Cook's Note: *Instead of drizzling chocolate with a spoon, warm chocolate may be spooned into a small plastic baggie, the corner snipped, and the chocolate squeezed over the brittle.*

Yield: 40 pieces

SUGAR COOKIES

I	cup butter
I	cup granulated sugar
I	large egg
I	teaspoon vanilla extract
2	teaspoons baking powder
3	cups all-purpose flour
I	teaspoon cinnamon
⅛	teaspoon nutmeg

Preheat oven to 400°. Cream butter and sugar in a large bowl with an electric mixer. Beat in egg and vanilla. In a separate bowl mix flour, cinnamon and nutmeg. Gradually add to butter mixture, mixing thoroughly after each addition. Dough will be very stiff. Divide into two portions. Roll dough on lightly floured surface to ⅛-inch thickness. Cut dough into desired shapes and bake on ungreased cookie sheets for 6-7 minutes. Remove cookies from pan and place on wire rack to cool.

FROSTING

½	cup unsalted butter, softened
4	cups confectioners' sugar
2	teaspoons vanilla extract
3-4	tablespoons milk

Cream butter and sugar in an electric mixer. Add vanilla and continue mixing. Add milk to thin to spreading consistency. Spread onto cookies using an off-set spatula or use piping bag to decorate as desired.

Cook's Note: *This frosting stays slightly soft, so use care when storing decorated cookies.*

Yield: 15-20 average size cookies

Marcel puts his cookies in little envelopes with the painting I did of him. He says, "That captures me more than anything else." So he uses that a lot for his advertising. In fact, he was my first inspiration for my chefs. He's so distinctive with his mustache.

MOLASSES COOKIES

- ¾ cup shortening or margarine
- 1 cup granulated sugar
- ¼ cup brown sugar
- ¼ cup unsulfered molasses
- 1 large egg
- 2 cups all-purpose flour
- 2 teaspoons baking soda
- ½ teaspoon ground cloves
- ½ teaspoon ground ginger
- ½ teaspoon salt
- 1 teaspoon ground cinnamon
- Granulated sugar

Cream together the shortening and the sugars. Add molasses, egg, flour, soda, cloves, ginger, salt, and cinnamon mixing well. Form into balls and roll in the granulated sugar. Place onto cookie sheets and bake at 375° for 8-10 minutes.

Yield: 4 dozen cookies

SOUTHERN PRALINES

- 1 cup brown sugar, packed
- 1 cup chopped pecans, toasted
- ¾ cup all-purpose flour
- ¼ cup butter, cut into small pieces
- 1 large egg, beaten
- 1 tablespoon rum
- 1 tablespoon vanilla extract
- Pinch of salt

Preheat oven to 350°. Line two baking sheets with parchment paper. In the bowl of an electric mixer, combine the sugar, pecans, flour, and butter. Mix gently until combined; the dough should resemble coarse crumbs. Add the egg, rum, vanilla, and salt and mix until combined. Drop cookies by teaspoonsful about 3 inches apart on the baking sheets. Bake 8-10 minutes until edges are golden brown. Place cookie sheet on a rack and cool for 10 minutes. Remove cookies from sheet and place directly on rack to finish cooling.

Yield: 48 cookies

KACEY'S HARLEQUIN PINWHEELS

PINWHEELS
- ¾ cup margarine, very soft
- 1½ cups light brown sugar
- 3 egg yolks
- 1½ teaspoons vanilla extract
- 3 cups all-purpose flour
- ¾ teaspoon baking powder

FILLING
- 3 tablespoons butter
- 3 cups semisweet chocolate chips
- 1 (14-ounce) can sweetened, condensed milk
- 3 teaspoons vanilla extract
- 1½ cups pecans, chopped and divided into thirds

Kacey Carneal is a highly creative artist and one of my favorites. She makes these fanciful pinwheel cookies that make me very happy.

Mix together margarine and sugar. Add egg yolks, vanilla, flour, and baking powder. Mix well. Divide dough into 3 parts and roll with rolling pin between 2 pieces of waxed paper. Shape into rectangles approximately 12x7 inches. In microwave, melt butter and chocolate chips together. Add condensed milk and vanilla. Divide into 3 parts. Spread ⅓ of filling on each of three dough rectangles. Sprinkle each rectangle with ⅓ of the nuts. Roll up rectangles from longest edge, lifting up waxed paper to help. When completely rolled, place in freezer. Slice frozen dough ¼-inch thick and bake on cookie sheets covered with foil at 350° for approximately 15 minutes. Have oven rack up one notch from bottom. Do not try to remove from the cookie sheets until completely cool.

Yield: 50 pinwheels

GOOD HOPES

CHOCOLATE CHEWS

- 8 ounces semisweet chocolate, finely chopped
- 3 ounces unsweetened chocolate, finely chopped
- 8 tablespoons butter, cut into small pieces
- 3 large eggs
- 1¼ cups granulated sugar
- 2 teaspoons vanilla extract
- ⅔ cup all-purpose flour
- ½ teaspoon baking powder
- ¼ teaspoon salt
- 1½ cups semisweet chocolate chips
- 1½ cups chopped walnuts
- 1½ cups chopped pecans

Set racks in upper and lower thirds of the oven. Preheat oven to 325°. Place chocolates and butter in a double boiler over barely simmering water. Stir occasionally until the chocolate and butter have melted. Set aside bowl to cool. In an electric mixer, whisk together the eggs and sugar for 3 minutes. Whisk in the melted chocolate mixture and the vanilla. In a separate bowl, combine the flour, baking powder and salt. Gently stir this mixture into the chocolate mixture. Stir in the chocolate chips and nuts. Drop tablespoon size mounds of batter onto parchment lined baking sheets 1-2 inches apart. Bake 12-15 minutes until the cookies are slightly firm and cracked. Cool cookies on pans until totally set, then transfer to a rack.

Yield: 5-6 dozen pieces

GERMAN CHOCOLATE LACE COOKIES

½   cup unsalted butter, room temperature
½   cup brown sugar, packed
2   tablespoons dark rum, divided
¼   cup heavy whipping cream
4   ounces semisweet chocolate, chopped
¼   cup all-purpose flour
⅛   teaspoon baking soda
¼   teaspoon salt
I   cup quick-cooking oats
½   cup shredded coconut
½   cup chopped pecans

Preheat oven to 350°. Grease and flour cookie sheets. Cream the butter and sugar in a mixer bowl for about 5 minutes or until light and fluffy. Beat in I tablespoon rum. Heat cream to boiling in a small saucepan. Reduce heat and stir in the remaining I tablespoon of rum. Simmer for 2-3 minutes. Remove from heat and stir in the chocolate until it melts and mixture is well blended. Beat ⅓ cup of the chocolate mixture into the butter mixture. Sift the flour, baking soda, and salt together. Stir into the butter mixture. Fold in the oats, coconut, and pecans. Drop rounded ½ teaspoons of the batter 2 inches apart onto the prepared cookie sheets. Bake for 8 minutes. Remove from oven and let cool on the cookie sheets for 5 minutes to harden. Remove cookies to wire racks to cool. Drizzle the remaining chocolate mixture over the cookies in a lacy pattern.

Yield: 40-50 cookies

LAURA'S AWESOME SHORTBREAD COOKIES

1	cup butter, softened
1	cup granulated sugar
2	large eggs
1	teaspoon vanilla extract
3	cups all-purpose flour
1½	teaspoons baking powder
½	teaspoon salt
	Cinnamon sugar or cookie sprinkles of choice

This past summer I made a painting I call "The Castle Club." It was a very elegant party with people dressed in tuxedos, at nighttime with candles. The other was "The Lawn Party" which was an outdoor party with a big cake. It's just a mood; it's like capturing a mood. I did one called "The House of Happiness" and it's a Thanksgiving

Preheat oven to 350°. In a large bowl cream butter and sugar. Add eggs and vanilla and mix well. Mix flour, baking powder, and salt together and add a little at a time into butter mixture. Mix completely. Roll dough out onto wax paper, about ¼-inch thick and place cookie sheet in freezer for about 15-20 minutes. Remove and cut with cookie cutters into desired shapes. Poke holes in cookies with toothpick. Sprinkle with cinnamon sugar or other decorations. If dough becomes too soft to work with, re-freeze about 10-15 minutes or until firm. Spray cookie sheet with cooking spray. Bake cookies for 8-10 minutes or until just brown around the edges. These cookies will not expand while baking.

Yield: 4 dozen cookies

CINNAMON BARS

- 1 cup unsalted butter, softened
- 1 cup granulated sugar
- 1 large egg, separated
- 2 tablespoons cinnamon
- 1 cup all-purpose flour
- 1 cup finely chopped pecans

Preheat oven to 325° and grease a 15½x10½-inch jelly-roll pan. In a bowl with an electric mixer beat the butter and sugar until light and fluffy. Beat in the egg yolk. Add cinnamon and flour beating until combined well. Spread dough evenly in pan. In a small bowl lightly beat egg white and brush dough with enough egg white to coat completely. Sprinkle pecans evenly over top and gently press them into the dough. Bake dough in middle of oven for 25 minutes or until golden brown. While confection is still warm, cut into bars, each about 2½x1½ inches and cool completely in pan on a rack.

Cook's Note: *These delectable cookies are at home from coffee time through tea time and dessert!*

Yield: 42 cookies

dinner. There really is a House of Happiness that my great aunt used to run. It was a home for underprivileged children and she ran it in Richmond. We would go there for Thanksgiving and she would always have this huge table with all this food and everything and that was the time the family could come to the House of Happiness.

212

CHOCOLATE CARAMEL BROWNIES

BROWNIE LAYER
- 4 ounces semisweet chocolate, chopped
- 1 ounce unsweetened chocolate, chopped
- ½ cup unsalted butter, cut into pieces
- 1 cup brown sugar, packed
- 1 teaspoon vanilla extract
- 2 large eggs
- ¾ cup plus 2 tablespoons all-purpose flour
- ¼ teaspoon baking powder
- ½ teaspoon salt

CARAMEL-PECAN LAYER
- ¾ cup granulated sugar
- ⅓ cup light corn syrup
- 3 tablespoons water
- Pinch of salt
- ⅓ cup heavy cream
- 1 teaspoon vanilla extract
- 1½ cups pecans

Preheat oven to 350°. Butter and flour a 9-inch square baking pan, knocking out all excess flour. Make the brownie layer first. In a heavy 1½-quart saucepan melt chocolate and butter over low heat, stirring until smooth. Remove pan from heat. Cool mixture to lukewarm and stir in brown sugar and vanilla. Add eggs, 1 at a time, beating well with a wooden spoon until mixture is glossy and smooth. In a bowl sift together flour, baking powder, and salt and add to chocolate mixture, beating just until batter is combined well. Spread batter evenly in pan and bake in middle of oven for 30-35 minutes, or until a tester comes out clean. Cool brownie layer completely in pan on a rack. Make the caramel-pecan layer. In a heavy 3-quart saucepan bring sugar, corn syrup, water, and a pinch of salt to a boil over moderate heat, stirring until sugar is dissolved. Boil mixture, without stirring, until it turns a golden caramel. Remove pan from heat and carefully add cream and vanilla (mixture will bubble up and steam). Stir in pecans and quickly pour mixture over brownie layer, spreading evenly.

Cool brownies completely in pan on a rack. Chill brownies, loosely covered, about 4 hours or until caramel is firm. Cut chilled brownies into 16 squares and remove from pan while still cold. Let brownies come to room temperature before eating.

Cook's Note: *Brownies will keep, covered and chilled in one layer, for 5 days.*

CHOCOLATE MINT BROWNIES

BOTTOM LAYER
1	cup butter or margarine
2	cups granulated sugar
1	teaspoon vanilla extract
4	large eggs
4	ounces unsweetened chocolate, melted
1	cup all-purpose flour

MIDDLE LAYER
2	cups confectioners' sugar
½	cup butter or margarine, softened
4	tablespoons green crème de menthe

TOP LAYER
6	ounces semisweet chocolate chips
6	tablespoons butter or margarine

Preheat oven to 325°. Cream the butter, sugar, and vanilla. Beat in the eggs. Blend in the melted chocolate. Gradually add the flour and stir. Pour the batter into a 9x12-inch greased pan. Bake for 20-25 minutes. Let cool. Combine all middle layer ingredients in a mixer and blend until smooth. Spread over the bottom layer. Melt the top layer ingredients together and spread on the top. Cool and cut into 2-inch squares.

Cook's Note: *These freeze beautifully.*

Yield: 40 brownies

214

WHITE CHOCOLATE BROWNIES

½ cup unsalted butter or margarine
8 ounces white chocolate chips or coarsely
 chopped white chocolate, divided
2 large eggs
 Pinch of salt
½ cup granulated sugar
½ teaspoon vanilla extract
½ teaspoon salt
1 cup all-purpose flour
8 ounces semisweet chocolate chips

Preheat oven to 350°. Lightly grease an 8-inch square pan. Line bottom with foil and lightly grease foil. Set pan aside. In a heavy saucepan, melt butter over low heat. Remove from heat and add half of white chocolate. Do not stir. In a large bowl, beat eggs and salt until frothy, using an electric mixer. Gradually add sugar, beating until pale yellow and a slowly dissolving ribbon forms when beaters are lifted. Combine butter mixture, vanilla, and salt. Add flour and mix until just combined. Stir in semisweet chocolate and remaining white chocolate. Spoon into prepared pan, smoothing top with a spatula. Bake 30 minutes. Cool in pan, and cut into squares.

Cook's Note: *May be made a day ahead.*

Yield: 16 brownies

Another story…
I did some angels and we painted them like the American flag, and this woman was wearing one when she got on a United Airlines flight; they gave her first class seat because they thought she was an employee!

VIENNESE RASPBERRY BARS

- 1¾ cups sweetened flaked coconut, divided
- 1¼ cups all-purpose flour
- ¾ cup light brown sugar, packed
- ¼ cup granulated sugar
- ½ teaspoon salt
- ¾ cup cold unsalted butter, cut into pieces
- 1½ cups old fashioned oats
- ¾ cup seedless raspberry jam

Preheat oven to 375°. Spread ¾ cup coconut evenly on a baking sheet and toast in middle of oven, stirring once, until golden, about 8 minutes. Cool. Blend together flour, sugars, and salt in a food processor. Add butter and blend until a dough begins to form. Transfer to a bowl and knead in oats and toasted coconut until combined well. Reserve ¾ cup dough. Press remainder evenly into bottom of a buttered 13x9-inch metal baking pan and spread jam over it. Crumble reserved dough evenly over jam, then sprinkle with remaining ¾ cup untoasted coconut. Bake in middle of oven for 20-25 minutes or until golden. Cool completely in pan on a rack. Loosen from sides of pan with a sharp knife, then lift out in 1 piece and transfer to a cutting board. Slice into bars.

Cook's Note: *Bars can be made 3 days ahead and kept in an airtight container at room temperature.*

Yield: 24 bars

APRICOT BARS

CRUST
½	cup butter, softened
I	cup all-purpose flour, sifted
¼	cup granulated sugar

FILLING
⅔	cup chopped, dried apricots
2	large eggs
I	cup brown sugar
⅓	cup sifted all-purpose flour
½	teaspoon baking powder
¼	teaspoon salt
½	teaspoon vanilla extract
½	cup chopped nuts
½	cup confectioners' sugar

Preheat oven to 350°. Mix butter, flour, and sugar together and press into bottom of greased 8x8-inch pan. Bake 25 minutes. Boil apricots in as little water as possible until soft. Set aside. Beat eggs well. Add brown sugar and flour, sifted together with baking powder and salt. Add vanilla and fold in drained apricots. Spread on top of baked crust and sprinkle with nuts. Bake for another 25 minutes until golden brown. Cut into squares and roll in confectioners' sugar.

Yield: 36 bars

KEY LIME BARS

1 ½ cups graham cracker crumbs
⅓ cup butter or margarine, melted
3 tablespoons granulated sugar
1 (8-ounce) package cream cheese, softened
14 ounces sweetened condensed milk
¼ cup Key lime juice or regular lime juice
1 tablespoon lime zest
Lime zest for garnish

Preheat oven to 350°. Grease bottom and sides of 9x9x2-inch square pan. Mix cracker crumbs, butter and sugar thoroughly with fork. Press evenly in bottom of pan. Refrigerate while preparing cream cheese mixture. Beat cream cheese in small bowl with electric mixer on medium speed until light and fluffy. Gradually beat in milk until smooth. Beat in lime juice and zest. Spread over layer in pan. Bake about 35 minutes or until center is set. Cool 30 minutes. Cover loosely and refrigerate at least 3 hours until chilled. Cut into bars and garnish with additional lime zest. Store covered in refrigerator.

Cook's Note: *If you love lemon, lemon juice and lemon zest may be substituted for the Key lime juice and zest.*

Yield: 36 bars

218

I'm not a big sweets person, but there have been times when I've had some chocolate that's just…well, it kind of melts you inside. It does something to your jaws and your body. It's a romantic feeling, an all-consuming feeling like love…fortunately, it's momentary!

FROZEN CHOCOLATE MINT VELVETS

½	cup butter
2	ounces unsweetened chocolate
1	cup confectioners' sugar
2	large eggs
½-¾	teaspoon mint extract
1	teaspoon vanilla extract

In a small saucepan, melt butter and add chocolate, stirring until melted and smooth. Add confectioners' sugar. In a mixer, beat eggs until well combined, then slowly add the chocolate mixture and the extracts. Beat 3-5 minutes or until smooth and fluffy. Pour into small demitasse cups or very small ramekins. Freeze until firm.

Cook's Note: *Elegant, nice, and yummy!*

Yield: 8-10 servings

CHOCOLATE CREAM POTS

1½	cups milk
2	large eggs, lightly beaten
2	cups semisweet chocolate chips
2	teaspoons rum
	Pinch of salt

Heat milk just to the boiling point. Put eggs, chocolate chips, rum and a pinch of salt in the container of a blender. Add hot milk and blend at low speed for 1 minute. Stir with a rubber spatula to remove any bubbles. Pour into 10 Pot de crème cups or demitasse cups and chill for several hours. Do not double the recipe.

Yield: 10 servings

YOGURT CREAM WITH RASPBERRY SAUCE

YOGURT CREAM
- 4 teaspoons unflavored gelatin
- 1/4 cup cold water
- 1 1/2 cups heavy cream, light cream or half-and-half
- 1/2 cup granulated sugar
- 2 1/2 cups plain yogurt
- 1 teaspoon vanilla extract

RASPBERRY SAUCE
- 1 tablespoon lemon juice
- Granulated sugar to taste
- 1 (20-ounce) package frozen raspberries

Mix gelatin and water and let soften for 10 minutes. Cook cream and sugar for 5 minutes, stirring constantly. Add gelatin and water mixture, remove from heat, and stir until gelatin is dissolved. Let cool 5 minutes and stir in yogurt and vanilla. Rinse a 1-quart decorative mold with cold water (don't dry it); pour in mixture and chill, loosely covered, for at least 2 1/2 hours. Run a thin knife around the edge of the mold. Dip in warm water and unmold with a sharp rap. Add lemon juice and sugar to frozen berries (fresh may be used) and mash slightly. Serve yogurt topped with raspberry sauce.

Cook's Note: *May be made in individual dishes.*

Yield: 8 servings

SIDNEY'S MOCHA WHISKEY CHOCOLATE MOUSSE TART

CRUST
- 1½ cups graham cracker crumbs
- ¼ cup brown sugar
- 1 ounce canola oil
- ½ cup unsweetened cocoa
- ½ cup confectioners' sugar

FILLINGS I & II
- 12 ounces semisweet chocolate, coarsely chopped
- 14 ounces heavy cream
- 6 ounces pecans, coarsely chopped
- ½ cup espresso
- 2 packages unflavored gelatin
- ½ cup granulated sugar
- 3 egg yolks, whisked
- 3 ounces bourbon
- 2 cups heavy cream

Sydney Mears is a wonderful chef, highly creative, and he gets passionate about it. With him, I'm a little bit further down the road with my taste buds. He'll have something special that he's created and he'll bring it out and say, "What do you think of this?" It's amazing how subtle some tastes can be, but if you're really paying attention, you can taste it. It's something you can learn.

In a medium bowl, combine graham cracker crumbs, brown sugar, canola oil, cocoa , and confectioners' sugar. Pat into a 9-inch springform pan or into 8 individual ramekins. Chill to set. In a medium bowl, mix together chocolate, heavy cream, and pecans. Microwave for 1½ minutes. Stir to combine and to melt the chocolate. This will be a nougat type of ganache. Set aside. Pour espresso into a small sauce pan, stirring in the gelatin to combine. In a small bowl, whisk together sugar and egg yolks. Stir into coffee gelatin mixture and place pan on low heat. Do not boil. Stir until gelatin is dissolved and mixture has thickened. Remove from heat and add bourbon. Set in an ice bath for a few minutes, stirring constantly to let cool, but not set. Remove from the ice bath. Whip the heavy cream to medium peaks. Fold into the coffee bourbon mixture and set aside. To assemble the tart, spoon the chocolate nut mixture onto the crust, spreading to 1-inch thickness. Top with the coffee mixture. Cover with plastic wrap and chill 6 hours or overnight. If desired, sprinkle with cocoa powder before serving.

Sydney Mears   *Yield: 8 servings*

SCRUMPTIOUS BERRY COBBLER

BERRY FILLING

6	cups fresh or frozen berries (blueberries, raspberries, blackberries)
¼	cup granulated sugar
1	tablespoon cornstarch
¼	teaspoon ground cinnamon
	Pinch of salt

TOPPING

1½	cups all-purpose flour
2	tablespoons granulated sugar
½	teaspoon baking soda
½	teaspoon baking powder
¼	teaspoon salt
4	tablespoons cold unsalted butter, cut into small bits
¾	cup low-fat buttermilk, well shaken
	Granulated sugar

Preheat oven to 425°. Mix all filling ingredients in a 2-quart heavy saucepan over moderate heat, stirring occasionally for about 2 minutes or until sugar begins to dissolve. Spoon filling into a 9-inch ceramic or glass pie plate .In the bowl of a food processor, blend together flour, sugar, baking soda, baking powder, and salt. Add butter bits and blend until mixture resembles coarse meal. Add buttermilk then pulse for about 10 seconds. (Do not over-mix.) Drop dough loosely in mounds over filling, leaving space between mounds. Sprinkle topping lightly with sugar. Bake for about 25 minutes or until topping is golden brown and fruit is bubbling. Cool slightly and serve warm with ice cream!

Yield: 8 servings

CRAN-APPLE BAKE

FILLING

12	ounces fresh cranberries
1½	cups sugar
5	tablespoons cornstarch
6-8	golden delicious apples, peeled, cored, and sliced
½	cup Cognac or bourbon

TOPPING

1	cup oatmeal
1	cup granulated sugar
1	cup walnuts or pecans, chopped
¼	cup all-purpose flour
8	tablespoons butter
1	tablespoon vanilla extract

The Alphabet of Sweets was such a fun project with Marcel. He wrote it all and came up with all the funny names and asked me if I would want to be a part of it and I said yes. It's a side of Marcel many people don't see. We had a lot of fun, going on tours and doing book signings. I wish we had pursued a second printing of the book.

Preheat oven to 350°. Spray a 9x13-inch baking pan with non-stick spray. Spread cranberries in the pan. Mix sugar and cornstarch, pour over cranberries, and stir. Place apples on top of cranberries. Pour the Cognac or bourbon on top of the apples. Mix together oatmeal, sugar, nuts, flour, butter, and vanilla. Spoon over apples. Bake uncovered for 1½ hours or until bubbly.

Cook's Note: *For cranberries any time of the year, freeze several bags when available in the fall and winter*

Yield: 8-12 servings

APPLE BAVARIAN TORTE

½ cup plus 1 tablespoon butter, chilled
3 green, tart apples, peeled, cored, and thinly sliced
⅓ cup brown sugar
½ teaspoon ground cinnamon
⅓ cup plus ¼ cup granulated sugar, chilled, divided
¼ teaspoon vanilla extract
1 cup all-purpose flour, chilled
1 (8-ounce) package cream cheese
1 tablespoon fresh lemon juice
½ teaspoon vanilla extract
1 tablespoon cornstarch
¼ cup sliced almonds

Preheat the oven to 400°. Grease a 9-inch springform pan. In a skillet over medium heat, melt 1 tablespoon butter. Toss the apples with the brown sugar and cinnamon and sauté for 2-3 minutes. Drain off and reserve the liquid. Cream together ½ cup butter, ⅓ cup sugar, ¼ teaspoon vanilla and the flour. Press the crust mixture into the bottom of the springform pan. Set aside. In a food processor, blend together the cream cheese, lemon juice, ½ teaspoon vanilla, cornstarch and remaining ¼ cup sugar. Pour this mixture over the crust and spread the apples on top. Bake for 10 minutes. Drizzle with a couple of spoonsful of the reserved apple liquid, avoiding the edges of the pan, and continue baking for 25 minutes. Sprinkle almonds over the top of the torte. Continue baking 5-10 minutes until lightly browned. Cool before removing from the pan.

Yield: 8 servings

224

GINGER-CREAM TART WITH RASPBERRIES

TART SHELL
- 2 cups ground shortbread cookies (two 5⅓-ounce packages)
- ¼ cup granulated sugar
- 3 tablespoons cold unsalted butter, cut into pieces

GINGER CREAM
- 1½ teaspoons unflavored gelatin
- 2 tablespoons milk
- ½ cup finely chopped crystallized ginger
- ¼ cup granulated sugar
- 1 teaspoon fresh lemon juice
- ¾ teaspoon salt
- 2 cups heavy cream, divided
- ¾ cup sour cream
- Confectioners' sugar and raspberries for garnish

Preheat oven to 350°. Blend ground shortbread, sugar, and butter in a food processor until mixture begins to clump together. Press into the bottom and up sides of a tart pan. Bake in the middle of the oven 15 minutes. Cool in the pan on a rack. Sprinkle gelatin over milk in a small bowl and let stand 1 minutes to soften. Transfer to a saucepan and cook with ginger, sugar, lemon juice, salt, and 1 cup heavy cream over moderate heat, stirring until sugar and gelatin are dissolved. Cool about 1 hour to room temperature. Whisk sour cream in a large bowl until smooth. Beat remaining cup of heavy cream in another bowl with an electric mixer until it just holds soft peaks and fold into sour cream. Gently fold ginger milk into whipped cream until combined well. Pour into crust and chill for at least 8 hours until set. Dust with confectioners' sugar and serve with raspberries

Cook's Note: *Tart can be chilled up to 1 day.*

Yield: 6-8 servings

CAPE COD CRANBERRY TORTE

2	cups cranberries
½	cup walnuts
½	cup granulated sugar
2	large eggs
¾	cup melted and cooled butter
1	cup granulated sugar
1	cup all-purpose flour
¼	teaspoon salt
¼	teaspoon almond extract

Preheat oven to 350°. In the bowl of the food processor, chop enough cranberries to make 2 cups and enough walnuts to make ½ cup. Pulse only to chop, not to purée. Place the cranberries and walnuts and ½ cup sugar in a greased 10-inch pie plate or spring form pan. Wipe out the processor bowl and add the eggs, melted butter, sugar, flour, salt, and extract. Mix until smooth and pour batter over the cranberry-walnut mixture. Bake 40 minutes or until a tester comes out clean. Serve warm with vanilla ice cream.

Cook's Note: *Cranberries freeze well and can be chopped while frozen.*

Yield: 8 servings

I hear so many stories about these little angels and where they go and the experiences people have when other people see them and how they affect their lives.

BREAD PUDDING

PUDDING

6	slices stale bread with crusts trimmed
3	tablespoons butter
½	cup seedless raisins
¾	cup granulated sugar
¾	teaspoon ground ginger
½	teaspoon cinnamon
¼	teaspoon salt
3	cups milk
I	teaspoon vanilla extract
3	large eggs

RUM BUTTER SAUCE

I	cup granulated sugar
2	tablespoons cornstarch
I	cup boiling water
½	cup lemon juice
	Zest of I lemon
½	cup butter
2	tablespoons brandy
¼	teaspoon nutmeg
½	cup light rum
2	tablespoons dark rum

Spread each slice of bread with butter. Place 2 slices in the bottom of greased 9x5x3-inch loaf pan. Add a layer of raisins. Repeat twice, using remaining butter, bread and raisins. Combine sugar, spices and salt with milk and vanilla. Beat eggs lightly and add to mixture. Pour over bread and raisins. Push bread into the liquid with back of a tablespoon, repeating often. Let stand 2 hours. Place in a pan of hot water. Bake in a preheated 325° oven I¼ hours until knife comes out clean. Blend sugar and cornstarch in boiling water. Cook over medium heat, stirring until it begins to thicken. Add to water, lemon juice, grated lemon rind, butter, brandy, nutmeg, and rums and cook 2 minutes, stirring constantly. Serve sauce on bread pudding.

Cook's Note: *Sauce may also be served over pound cake.*

Yield: 8 servings; 3 cups of sauce

MISSISSIPPI MUD CAKE

CAKE

1	cup butter, melted
2	cups granulated sugar
½	cup unsweetened cocoa
4	large eggs, lightly beaten
1	teaspoon vanilla extract
⅛	teaspoon salt
1½	cups all-purpose flour
1½	cups coarsely chopped pecans, toasted
1	(10½-ounce) bag miniature marshmallows

FROSTING

1	(16-ounce) package confectioners' sugar, sifted
½	cup milk
¼	cup butter, softened
⅓	cup unsweetened cocoa

Preheat oven to 350°. Whisk together melted butter, sugar, cocoa, eggs, vanilla, and salt in a large bowl. Stir in flour and chopped pecans. Pour batter into a greased and floured 15x10-inch jelly-roll pan. Bake for 20 to 25 minutes or until a wooden pick inserted in center comes out clean. While the cake is baking, make the chocolate frosting by beating the sugar, milk, butter, and cocoa together at medium speed with an electric mixer until smooth. This makes 2 cups of frosting. Remove the cake from the oven and top warm cake evenly with marshmallows. Return to oven and bake 5 minutes. Drizzle chocolate frosting over the warm cake. Cool completely.

Yield: 15 servings

NANCY'S "ANGEL" CAKE

6 large egg yolks, reserving the whites for the frosting
1 cup whole milk, divided
2¼ teaspoons vanilla
3 cups sifted cake flour
1½ cups granulated sugar
4 teaspoons baking powder
¾ teaspoon salt
12 tablespoons butter

My wonderful staff had this cake made for me to celebrate the 25th anniversary of my gallery shop. They commissioned chef Leslie Anderson to make it look just like my Angel Cake painting! Sometimes I paint cakes and sometimes I just eat cake!

Preheat oven to 350°. Grease two 9x1½-inch cake pans. Line bottoms with wax paper and grease and flour the lined pans. In a medium bowl lightly combine the egg yolks, ¼-cup milk, and vanilla. In a large mixing bowl combine the flour, sugar, baking powder, and salt and mix on low speed for 30 seconds to blend. Add the butter and remaining ¾-cup milk. Mix on low speed until the ingredients are moistened. Increase to medium speed (high speed if using a hand mixer) and beat for 1½ minutes. Scrape down sides. Gradually add the egg mixture in 3 batches, beating for 20 seconds after each addition. Scrape the batter into the prepared pans and smooth the surface with a spatula. The pans will be about ½ full. Bake 25-35 minutes or until a tester inserted near the center comes out clean and the cake springs back when pressed lightly in the center. Cool cakes on a rack for 10 minutes. Loosen the sides with a small metal spatula and invert onto wire racks. To prevent splitting, re-invert so tops are up. Cool completely before frosting.

Yield: Two 9-inch cakes

BUTTERCREAM FROSTING

1¼ cups granulated sugar, divided
⅜   cup water
6   large egg whites
¾   teaspoon cream of tartar
2½ cups unsalted butter, softened but cool
½   cup crème de cacao

In a medium size heavy saucepan stir together 1 cup sugar with the water. Over high heat, stir constantly until sugar dissolves and the syrup is bubbling. Stop stirring when it starts to boil and turn down the heat to simmer. In a mixing bowl beat egg whites until foamy, add the cream of tartar, and beat until soft peaks form. Gradually beat in remaining ¼-cup sugar until stiff peaks form when beater is raised. Using a candy thermometer, check the temperature of the syrup. When it reaches 248-250°, immediately remove from the heat and beat the syrup into the egg whites in a steady stream, slowly, until all syrup is incorporated. Beat until mixture is cool, about 5 minutes. Beat in butter at medium speed, 1 tablespoon at a time, until all butter is incorporated and the mixture has thickened. Lower the beater speed and gradually drizzle in the crème de cacao. Frost cakes.

Cook's Note: Buttercream becomes spongy upon standing so re-beat to maintain silky texture. This recipe makes enough to frost and decorate two 9-inch 2-layer cakes. Freeze unused portion for up to 8 months. Allow frozen buttercream to come to room temperature before using.

Leslie Anderson   *Yield: 3 cups*

APPLE CAKE WITH CREAM CHEESE FROSTING

CAKE

4	cups peeled, cored and diced apples
2	large eggs, slightly beaten
2	cups granulated sugar
2	teaspoons cinnamon
½	cup canola oil
1	cup chopped walnuts
2	cups all-purpose flour
2	teaspoons baking soda
¾	teaspoon salt

FROSTING

1	(8-ounce) package cream cheese, softened
3¾	cups confectioners' sugar
2	tablespoons milk
1	teaspoon vanilla extract

Preheat oven to 350°. Grease and flour a 13x9-inch pan. In a large bowl combine apples, eggs, sugar, cinnamon, oil, and nuts. In a small bowl combine flour, baking soda, and salt. Add to the apple mixture and mix until well combined. Pour the batter into the pan and bake for 55 minutes. While cake is baking, prepare the frosting. In a bowl with a mixer, beat cream cheese for a minute. Add confectioners' sugar, milk, and vanilla. Beat 2 minutes or until frosting is smooth and light. When the cake has cooled, frost with the cream cheese frosting or simply shake some confectioners' sugar on top. Makes 2 cups of frosting or enough to frost a 2-layer cake or one 13x9-inch cake.

Yield: 12 servings

LEMON BLUEBERRY POUND CAKE

CAKE
- ⅓ cup milk
- 6 large eggs
- 1½ tablespoons vanilla extract
- 2⅔ cups all-purpose flour
- 1 teaspoon double-acting baking powder
- 1¼ teaspoons salt
- 1½ cups unsalted butter, softened
- ½ cup granulated sugar
- ¾ cup firmly packed light brown sugar
- ¼ cup lemon zest
- 3 cups blueberries, tossed with 1½ tablespoons all-purpose flour

SYRUP
- ⅓ cup fresh lemon juice
- ½ cup granulated sugar

Preheat oven to 350°. In a small bowl whisk together milk, eggs, and vanilla. Into a bowl sift together the flour, baking powder, and the salt. In a large bowl with an electric mixer, cream the butter with the sugars and the zest until the mixture is light and fluffy. Add the flour mixture alternately with the egg mixture, beginning and ending with the flour mixture and beating the batter after each addition until it is just combined. Fold in 1½ cups of the blueberries. Spoon one third of the batter into a greased and floured 10-inch (3-quart) Bundt pan, spreading it evenly, and sprinkle ½ cup of the remaining blueberries over it. Repeat this procedure twice. Bake the cake in the middle of a preheated 350° oven for 1 hour to 1 hour and 10 minutes or until it is golden and a tester comes out clean. Make the syrup while the cake is baking. In a small saucepan combine lemon juice and sugar. Bring the mixture to a boil, stirring until the sugar is dissolved. Remove the pan from the heat. Remove the cake from the oven, poke the top immediately all over with a wooden skewer, and brush it with half the syrup. Let the cake cool in the pan on a rack for 10 minutes. Remove from pan and invert it onto a rack and poke it all over with the skewer. Brush the cake with the remaining syrup and let it cool completely.

Yield: 12 servings

LEMON CAKE

CAKE

½	pound unsalted butter, softened
2½	cups granulated sugar, divided
4	extra-large eggs at room temperature
⅓	cup lemon zest (6 to 8 large lemons)
3	cups all-purpose flour
½	teaspoon baking powder
½	teaspoon baking soda
1	teaspoon Kosher salt
¾	cup freshly squeezed lemon juice, divided
¾	cup buttermilk at room temperature
1	teaspoon vanilla extract

GLAZE

2	cups confectioners' sugar
3½	tablespoons freshly squeezed lemon juice

I painted cakes because I wanted to decorate cakes. My alternative to decorating cakes was to paint them.

Preheat oven to 350°. Grease two 8½x4½x2½-inch loaf pans. Cream the butter and 2 cups sugar in the bowl of an electric mixer for about 5 minutes, or until light and fluffy. With the mixer on medium speed, add eggs, one at a time, with the lemon zest. Sift together the flour, baking powder, baking soda, and salt in a bowl. In another bowl, combine ¼ cup lemon juice, buttermilk, and vanilla. Add the flour and buttermilk mixtures alternately to the batter, beginning and ending with the flour. Divide the batter evenly between the pans, smooth the tops, and bake for 45 minutes to 1 hour or until a cake tester comes out clean. Mix together the confectioners' sugar and lemon juice and spread on warm loaves.

Yield: two 8-inch loaves

ORANGE CARROT CAKE

CAKE
- ½ cup walnuts, chopped
- 2 cups carrots, grated
- 1 large orange, peel left on, quartered, puréed
- 2 cups all-purpose flour
- 2 cups granulated sugar
- 2 teaspoons baking powder
- 2 teaspoons baking soda
- 2 teaspoons cinnamon
- 2 teaspoons nutmeg
- 1 teaspoon salt
- 1¼ cups vegetable oil
- 4 large eggs
- ½ cup raisins

CREAM CHEESE ICING
- 1 (8-ounce) package cream cheese
- 2 tablespoons honey
- ½ teaspoon vanilla extract

Preheat the oven to 350°. Prepare walnuts, carrots and orange purée in a food processor. Mix together the flour, sugar, baking powder, baking soda, cinnamon, nutmeg, and salt. Add the orange purée, oil, and eggs. Mix thoroughly. Blend in the carrots, nuts, and raisins. Grease and flour a tube cake pan. Pour in mixture and bake for 1 hour. While cake is baking, make icing Soften the cream cheese and blend with honey and vanilla to taste. Spread on top of the cooled cake. Double the icing recipe to ice the sides, if desired.

Yield: 12 servings

234

ORANGE CHOCOLATE CHUNK CAKE

CAKE
- ½ pound unsalted butter, softened
- 2 cups granulated sugar
- 4 extra-large eggs at room temperature
- ¼ cup grated orange zest (4 large oranges)
- 3 cups all-purpose flour
- ½ teaspoon baking powder
- ½ teaspoon baking soda
- 1 teaspoon Kosher salt
- ¼ cup freshly squeezed orange juice
- ¾ cup buttermilk at room temperature
- 1 teaspoon vanilla extract
- 2 cups semisweet chocolate chunks, tossed with 2 tablespoons all-purpose flour

SYRUP
- ¼ cup granulated sugar
- ¼ cup freshly squeezed orange juice

GANACHE
- 8 ounces semisweet chocolate chips
- ½ cup heavy cream
- 1 teaspoon instant coffee granules

Preheat oven to 350°. Grease and flour a 10-inch Bundt pan. Cream the butter and sugar with an electric mixer for about 5 minutes or until light and fluffy. Add the eggs, one at a time. Add the orange zest. Sift together 3 cups flour, baking powder, baking soda, and salt in a large bowl. In another bowl, combine the orange juice, buttermilk, and vanilla. Add the flour and buttermilk mixtures alternately in thirds to the creamed butter, beginning and ending with the flour. Toss the chocolate chunks with 2 tablespoons flour and add to the batter. Pour into the pan, smooth the top, and bake for 45 minutes to 1 hour, or until a cake tester comes out clean. Let the cake cool in the pan on a wire rack for 10 minutes. Prepare the syrup. In a small saucepan over medium-low heat, cook the sugar with the orange juice until the sugar dissolves. Remove the cake from the pan, set it on a rack over a tray, and spoon the orange syrup over the cake. Allow the cake to cool completely. For the ganache, melt the chocolate, heavy cream, and coffee in the top of a double boiler over simmering water until smooth and warm, stirring occasionally. Drizzle over the top of the cake.

Yield: 12 servings

CREAM CHEESE POUND CAKE

1½	cups butter
1	(8-ounce) package cream cheese, softened
3	cups granulated sugar
6	large eggs
3	cups all-purpose flour
⅛	teaspoon salt
1	tablespoon vanilla extract
1	teaspoon lemon extract

Preheat oven to 300°. Beat butter and cream cheese at medium speed with an electric mixer until creamy. Gradually add sugar, beating well. Add eggs, one at a time, beating until combined. Combine flour and salt and gradually add to butter mixture, beating at low speed just until blended. Stir in vanilla and lemon extract. Pour into greased and floured 10-inch Bundt pan. Bake for 1 hour and 40 minutes (check at 1 hour 30 minutes) or until tester inserted in center comes out clean. Cool in pan on a wire rack 10-15 minutes. Remove from pan and let cool completely on wire rack.

Cook's Note: *Serve plain or with ice cream or berries. This freezes beautifully.*

Yield: 12 servings

CHOCOLATE RASPBERRY PUDDING CAKE

FROSTING
- ½ cup seedless raspberry jam
- ½ cup heavy cream
- 3 ounces good bittersweet chocolate (not unsweetened), chopped

CAKE BATTER
- ½ cup boiling water
- ⅓ cup plus 2 teaspoons unsweetened cocoa powder (not Dutch-process)
- ¼ cup whole milk
- ½ teaspoon vanilla extract
- ⅓ cup seedless raspberry jam
- I cup all-purpose flour
- ¾ teaspoon baking soda
- ¼ teaspoon salt
- 8 tablespoons unsalted butter, softened
- ⅓ cup packed light brown sugar
- ⅓ cup granulated sugar
- 2 large eggs
- Raspberries for garnish

I'll tell you who makes some of the most wonderful sweets and that's Rowena Fullinwider. I'm not a cake eater, but some of hers are just heaven.

Preheat oven to 350°. Generously butter 9x2-inch cake pan. Make frosting, by combining jam, cream, and chocolate in a small heavy saucepan and bring just to a simmer, stirring occasionally until smooth. Pour frosting into buttered cake pan. Make the cake batter by whisking together boiling water and cocoa powder in a medium bowl until smooth. Whisk in milk, vanilla, and jam. Sift together flour, baking soda, and salt into another bowl. Beat together butter and sugars in a large bowl with an electric mixer at medium-high speed until pale and fluffy. Add eggs one at a time, beating well after each addition. Add flour and cocoa mixtures alternately in batches, beginning and ending with flour mixture, beating on low speed until each addition is incorporated. Spoon batter evenly over frosting covering frosting completely. Bake 30 to 40 minutes (frosting on bottom will still be liquid). Cool cake in pan on a rack for 10 to 20 minutes. Run a thin knife around edge of pan and twist pan gently back and forth on a flat surface to loosen cake. Invert a cake plate with a slight lip over pan and, holding pan and plate together with both hands, invert cake onto plate. (Frosting will cover sides of cake and run onto plate.) Serve warm, garnished with raspberries, if desired.

Cook's Note: *The cake can be made up to 1 day ahead, cooled completely in the pan, kept in the pan, covered, at room temperature. Reheat the cake, uncovered, in a 350° oven for 15 minutes, then invert onto a plate as directed above.*

Yield: 6-8 servings

CHOCOLATE BOURBON PECAN PIE

4	large eggs
3	tablespoons butter, melted
⅔	cup granulated sugar
⅔	cup packed brown sugar
⅓	cup light corn syrup
3	tablespoons pure maple syrup
2	tablespoons bourbon
1	teaspoon vanilla extract
1	(9-inch) uncooked deep dish pie shell
⅔	cup semisweet chocolate chips
1	cup pecans chopped

Preheat oven to 400°. In a large bowl, beat eggs with an electric mixer on medium speed. Add butter and continue to beat until well blended. Add sugars and blend into a smooth mixture. Stir in corn syrup, maple syrup, bourbon, and vanilla. Set aside. Line the pie shell with the chocolate chips. Pour in the filling mixture. Arrange chopped pecans neatly over the filling. Place pie in oven and reduce the heat to 275°. Bake 1-1½ hours.

Cook's Note: *This is very rich. Cut into small pieces. May be served with vanilla ice cream.*

Yield: 10 servings

BEACH WEEK CHOCOLATE CARAMEL PIE

CRUST
- ½ cup pecan pieces, toasted and coarsely chopped
- 1 (6-ounce) chocolate-flavored crumb pie crust

CARAMEL LAYER
- ¾ cup individually wrapped caramels (17 squares), unwrapped
- ¼ cup evaporated milk (not sweetened condensed)

TRUFFLE LAYER
- 1½ cups semisweet chocolate chips
- 1 cup heavy whipping cream
- 3 tablespoons butter

OPTIONAL GARNISH
- 1 cup heavy cream beaten to stiff peaks, sweetened with 1 tablespoon granulated sugar

Sprinkle pecans on pie crust. Heat caramels and evaporated milk in a heavy saucepan over low heat or in a bowl in microwave, stirring often until caramels melt and mixture is smooth. Pour over pecans in crust. Make the truffle layer by heating chocolate chips, cream, and butter in a heavy saucepan over low heat or in a bowl in microwave, stirring until chocolate melts and mixture is smooth. Pour over caramel layer and refrigerate about 4 hours or until set. If desired, pipe or spoon on whipped cream.

Cook's Note: *Take all the ingredients to the beach and assemble after breakfast for a special after-dinner treat.*

Yield: 8 servings

It's unbelievable. I don't want to get too hokey, but I feel like I'm a vessel or something, like it's coming through me because sometimes I'll look at things I've painted and I'll think, how did I do that? How did I, Nancy Thomas, do that? I couldn't have done it alone.

STRAWBERRY PIE

I	quart hulled strawberries, divided
3	tablespoons cornstarch
I	cup granulated sugar
2	tablespoons lemon juice
I	baked 9-inch pie shell
½-¾	cup heavy cream
	Granulated sugar to taste
	Vanilla extract to taste

Place one half of hulled berries in food processor and pulse to medium chop (do not purée). Place chopped berries into saucepan and stir in cornstarch, sugar and lemon juice. Cook slowly over moderate heat, stirring constantly until thickened and clear. Cool for 1 hour in refrigerator. Cut remaining berries in half and stir them into cooled strawberry mixture. Turn into cooked pie crust. Whip the heavy cream with sugar and vanilla and spread over entire pie. Return to refrigerator until ready to serve.

Cook's Note: *This pie is easy and quick to make and may be served the same day it is made.*

Yield: 8 servings

CREAMY FRESH KUMQUAT PIE

I	(9-inch) baked pie shell
I	(8-ounce) package cream cheese, softened
¾	cup granulated sugar
I	teaspoon lemon oil
2	cups heavy cream, whipped
I	cup freshly puréed kumquats
I	cup thinly sliced kumquats

Bake and cool pie shell and set aside. In a small bowl, whisk together cream cheese, sugar, and lemon oil. Fold in whipped cream and kumquat purée. Spread into baked pie shell. Cover and refrigerate. Just before serving, cover the top with kumquat slices.

Cook's Note: *This recipe, a favorite of Nancy Thomas, from her daughter, artist, Hunter Thomas, may be made one day in advance.*

FROZEN KEY LIME PIE

CRUST
- 1½ cups graham cracker crumbs
- 1 tablespoon granulated sugar
- 4 tablespoons butter or margarine

FILLING
- 1 (14-ounce) can sweetened condensed milk
- ½ cup Key lime juice
- 2 cups heavy or whipping cream, divided
- Lime zest for garnish

Preheat oven to 350°. Combine graham cracker crumbs with sugar and butter, mixing well. Press into 9-inch pie plate. Combine sweetened condensed milk and lime juice in a large bowl and stir. Beat 1 cup of cream to stiff peaks. Fold into milk mixture until blended. Scoop filling into prepared crust. Garnish with lime zest. Freeze until semi-firm, at least 4 hours. Let stand at room temperature for 10 minutes before serving. Top with the second cup of cream, beaten to stiff peaks.

Cook's Note: *Less sweet than the usual, this frozen version of Key lime pie is simplicity at its best.*

Yield: 8 servings

My mother taught me never to brag about myself. If you're doing a good job, other people will talk about you. So I never said anything and my mother never said anything around me. You know, she never said my daughter is an artist or anything. So one day, unbeknownst to me, she had a friend over and she was bragging about my artistic ability and she ran into my bedroom and she grabbed a stack of papers, little drawings I'd been doing, to show to her friend, and the drawing on top was of a little girl cowed in the corner with the mother looming over her…she said she was so mortified!

FROZEN CHOCOLATE COFFEE PIE

CRUST
2	cups Oreo cookie crumbs
¼	cup butter, softened

SAUCE
3	(1-ounce) squares unsweetened chocolate
¼	cup butter
⅔	cup granulated sugar
	Dash of salt
⅔	cup evaporated milk
1	teaspoon vanilla extract

FILLING
2	pints coffee ice cream, softened

TOPPING
1	cup whipping cream
3	tablespoons confectioners' sugar
1	cup chopped nuts (optional)

Combine cookie crumbs and soft butter and press into the bottom of a 10-inch pie plate. Freeze. Melt chocolate squares, butter, sugar, and salt in the top of a double boiler, stirring constantly. Gradually add milk, blending well. Add vanilla. Cool and chill. Spoon softened ice cream into crust. Spoon chocolate sauce over ice cream and freeze. To complete pie, beat the whipping cream, adding confectioners' sugar and beating until stiff. Top pie with whipped cream and chopped nuts, if desired. Freeze. Before serving, allow pie to stand at room temperature for 20-30 minutes.

Yield: 8-10 servings

242

STRAWBERRIES WITH BROWN SUGAR AND BALSAMIC VINEGAR

- 2 cups small strawberries, halved, hulled
- 2 tablespoons brown sugar
- 1½ tablespoons balsamic vinegar
- ⅛ teaspoon black pepper
  - Vanilla ice cream or vanilla frozen yogurt
  - Mint leaves for garnish

Combine strawberries, sugar, vinegar, and pepper in a bowl. Cover and marinate in refrigerator for 20 minutes. Serve over vanilla ice cream or vanilla frozen yogurt and garnish with mint leaves.

Cook's Note: *While novel in the United States, this dessert is a staple in Italy. The sum is much greater than its parts! Serve on Italian pottery leaf plates or in stemmed goblets.*

Yield: 4 servings

SUMMER SURPRISE DESSERT

- 1 cup fresh seedless grapes, halved
- 1 cup fresh whole blueberries
- 1 cup fresh strawberries, halved, hulled
- 1 cup fresh peaches, cut in bite-sized pieces
- 1 cup firmly packed brown sugar
- 2 cups sour cream

In a shallow 9x12-inch glass dish, combine all fruit and mix well. Sprinkle brown sugar over the fruit. Top with sour cream. Cover with plastic wrap and refrigerate 3 to 4 hours or overnight. The sour cream will seep through the brown sugar to the fruit. To serve, gently stir the fruit and spoon into sherbet glasses.

Cook's Note: *Any combination of fresh fruits may be used.*

I was doing angels and I was experimenting with the wings and I didn't want to paint a white angel so I painted a red one. I was showing in New York then. The set decorators of the movie Tootsie were going around leasing things to decorate the sets with. So they came in to Mary Emmerling's shop and leased 35 of my pieces and that angel was one of them, but I knew some of them were in the movie. So I went to the movie and there was that angel in one of the major scenes in the movie where Dustin

HONEY BALSAMIC ROASTED PEARS

2   tablespoons unsalted butter
2   firm, ripe Bosc pears, halved lengthwise
        and cored
3   tablespoons balsamic vinegar
¼   pound Manchego or mild fresh goat
        cheese, cut into 4 pieces, at room
        temperature
¼   cup honey
        Freshly ground black pepper

Preheat oven to 400°. Place butter in an 8-inch square baking dish and melt in oven for about 3 minutes. Arrange pears, cut sides down, in one layer in dish. Roast for 20 minutes or until tender. Pour vinegar over pears and roast for 5 minutes more. Transfer pears, cut sides down, to serving plates and spoon some of juices from baking dish over them. Arrange cheese next to pears, drizzle pears and cheese with honey, and sprinkle with pepper.

Cook's Note: Pears surrounded by chunks of cheese and served with a dish of honey are a very Italian ending to a meal. This recipe embellishes the idea by roasting the pears with vinegar to sharpen the flavor, setting them beside the cheese, and drizzling honey across the top. A little black pepper adds sparkle.

Yield: 4 servings

Hoffman was trying to tell Jessica Lange that he was a man. The scene kept going back and forth and there was that angel. That was the funniest feeling in the world to see your artwork on a big screen like that. Anyhow, they ended up buying everything and I met Dustin Hoffman…it was just one of those things that happened.

244

ROASTED PEARS WITH SESAME SEEDS

2	teaspoons unsalted butter, cut into bits
4	firm, ripe Bosc pears, peeled, halved lengthwise, and cored
1	tablespoon fresh lemon juice
3	tablespoons water
1½	tablespoons granulated sugar
¼	teaspoon Chinese five-spice powder
2	teaspoons sesame seeds, toasted

Preheat oven to 375°. Grease an 11x7-inch glass or ceramic baking dish with some of the butter. Brush pears all over with lemon juice and place, cut sides down, into baking dish. Pour water around pears and scatter remaining butter in dish. Sprinkle pears with sugar and five-spice powder. Bake, uncovered, in middle of oven for 15 to 20 minutes, brushing frequently with pan juices, until pears are tender and golden brown. Serve pears warm, drizzled with some pan juices and sprinkled with sesame seeds.

Yield: 4 servings

I was commissioned to do the official White House Christmas tree. There were seven of us artists that they commissioned to do ornaments and we all had a reception with Nancy Reagan. That was extremely wonderful.

INDEX

254

V

VEAL

W

Y

Z

ZUCCHINI, *See Squash*

Ship To: (if different address)
Name _____

Address _____

City _____ State _____ Zip _____

Telephone (___) _____

Method of Payment _____

[   ] Check payable to Peninsula Fine Arts Center

[   ] VISA   [   ] MasterCard

Name (as it appears on card) _____

Card Number _____ Expiration Date _____

Signature _____

	QUANTITY	AMOUNT DUE
Art of the Palette at $24.95 per book	_____	_____
Art of the Palette at $299.40 per case of 12	_____	_____

Shipping and Handling _____

$4.00 for first book; $2.00 for each additional book **OR**
    $10.00 per case   _____

Subtotal   _____

Sales Tax (Virginia residents add 5.5% on Subtotal. No tax if mailing out of state.)   _____

TOTAL   _____

Mail Order Form to: Peninsula Fine Arts Center
                          101 Museum Drive
                          Newport News, Virginia 23606

Telephone: (757) 596-8175

Fax Order Form to: (757) 596-0807

Send Via Email to: www.PFAC.VA.org

                    Photocopies will be accepted.